sex

REDISCOVERING DESIRE
THROUGH TECHNIQUES &
THERAPIES

sex

REDISCOVERING DESIRE THROUGH TECHNIQUES & THERAPIES

ALIZA BARON COHEN

TAYLOR TRADE PUBLISHING
Lanham • New York • Dallas • Boulder • Toronto •Oxford

Published by Taylor Trade Publishing
An imprint of The Rowman & Littlefield Publishing Group, Inc.
4501 Forbes Boulevard, Suite 200
Lanham, Maryland 20706

First published in Great Britain in 2005 by
Kyle Cathie Limited
122 Arlington Road London NW1 7HP

Distributed by National Book Network

Library of Congress Card Number: 2004115763
ISBN 1 58979 217 3   (alk. paper)

The paper used in this publication meets the minimum requirements of American National Standard for Information Sciences—Permanence of Paper for Printed Library Materials, ANSI/NISO Z39.48–1992.

Text © 2005 Aliza Baron Cohen
Photography © 2005 John Davis
(For additional photography credits, see page 143.)
The Invitation (poem) © 1999 Oriah Mountain Dreamer

Project editor Sarah Epton
Editorial assistant Vicki Murrell
Proofreader Ruth Baldwin
Designer Heidi Baker
Recipes Vanessa Kendell
Production Sha Huxtable and Alice Holloway

Aliza Baron Cohen is hereby identified as the author of this work in accordance with Section 77 of the Copyright, Designs and Patents Act 1988.

A CIP record for this title is available from the British Library.

Colour separations by Scanhouse, Malaysia
Printed and bound by Kyodo, Singapore

Note: if you are taking any prescription drugs or have a serious health condition please check with your doctor before you use any herbal or vitamin supplement, as they may cause an adverse reaction.

Dosages are generally not given in this book, as they may vary from person to person. If a recommended dosage is not stated on the product itself, it is advised that you seek the help of a herbalist, homeopath or qualified health practitioner before taking any herbal or vitamin supplements.

The herbal tonic recipes, 'Adventures of Adam' and 'Eve of Romance' are included with the kind permission of Jeff Stein and Edgar Veytia, authors of the book *Elixir's, Tonics and Teas*.

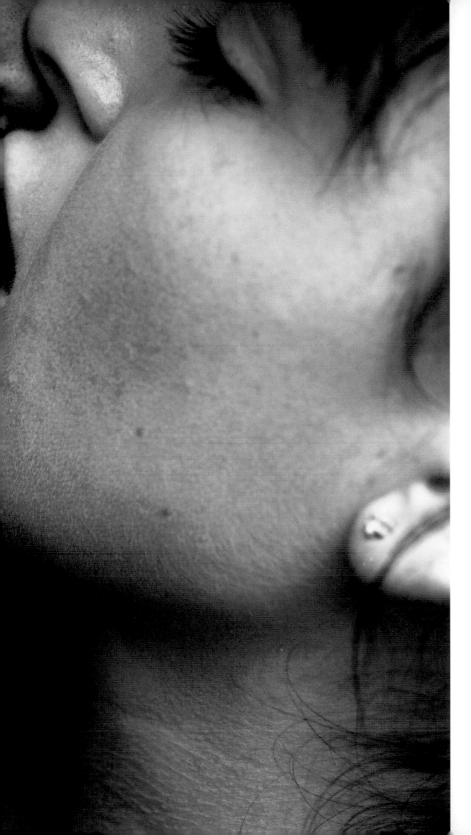

Author's acknowledgements

I'd like to thank my husband, for the support he always gives me when I'm writing my books, my daughter Shayna and my son Kobi for being patient with me when waiting for their bedtime stories and goodnight kisses. And for the laughter and love they always bring to my day.

I couldn't have written this book without Helen, my friend and business partner, who let me 'borrow' her flat and who kept the business going throughout my absence.

I'd like to thank the 'gunge queen' Leaanne for her eternal positivity and continual support through my many crises. Also to Kate 'the dance goddess' who introduced me to dancing and the many ways it can help to improve intimacy and increase libido. Thanks to Mike, Mark and Mark for their humor and male perspective on things.

Thanks to all the Bliss crew, especially Hari and Adrian who helped supply the herbal sex tonic recipes, and Dani, Jo, Jo, Asaf, and all the fantastic therapists who kept me going with humour, massage, and psychotherapy!

Thanks to my publisher, Kyle Cathie and the creative team: Sarah Epton, Heidi Baker, John Davis, models Fifi Russo, Richard Robinson, Abigail Toyne, Lena Franks, and Alan Reeves, and also Vanessa Kendell for her delicious aphrodisiac recipes.

Last but not least, big thanks as always to my parents for their love and advice and my brothers Ash, Si, and Dan for their eternal guidance and love. A special thanks to my mum for her contributions to all my books and for her openness, which has enabled me to be the woman I am today.

contents

introduction

"If sex is such a natural phenomenon, how come there are so many books on how to do it?" Bette Midler

Sex. Everyone is fascinated by it at some point in their life, some are obsessed by it and spend their lives pursuing it, and some are frightened by the very thought of it. Considering that sex and sexuality have been a preoccupation of every culture throughout history, you would think we would be experts on the subject by now, yet it still continues to confuse us. Working in the health field, I get to talk to people with a variety of problems, both physical and psychological. In my experience, a common complaint among people of all ages is a low or complete lack of libido. It is often something that people find hard to talk about; in fact, they generally come to see me about something else but soon bring it up. Yet it is nothing to be embarrassed about. It can affect us all at some time in our life.

It was an ancient belief that if you were able to have a healthy libido, you were in good overall health. I would add also that if you are in poor health it's more than likely you won't have a good sex drive. This doesn't mean just poor physical health but also emotional and spiritual health, too. And too strong a sex drive is just as much an indication of a health imbalance as a weak libido, or none at all.

As with most physical problems, there are many possible causes, but thankfully many effective ways it can be treated. I hope this book answers some of the questions you may have and helps you discover the solution you seek to help you reclaim what is rightfully yours: the desire for passion. Remember, human beings are one of the few species that are able to enjoy sex for both procreation and recreation!

Before we look at what the libido is and why it can start to wane, let's consider some of the ways different cultures have viewed sex in the past. It will become apparent that many of our problems today are inextricably linked with our cultural history of repression as well as with the society we now live in, in which we are bombarded with sexual images all the time. Perhaps by looking at how sex was regarded at other times and by other peoples, we may be able to look afresh at sexual desire with a different, healthier perspective.

A short history of sex

In prehistoric times depictions of people having sex were scratched onto rocks and cave walls, and representations of both male and female genitals were carved from stone and wood. Fertility—often symbolized by the erect penis—was crucial to human survival, and not only the fertility of humans but of

An erotic wall fresco from first-century Rome.

crops and livestock as well. The generative process was thus venerated by many peoples all over the world.

Fascination with sex was not confined to primitive cultures, however. The ancient Egyptians, Greeks, and Romans were also preoccupied by it, and much of their mythology recounts tales of desire and passion, incest, rape, adultery, and union between the most unlikely partners. Nor was their interest limited to flights of fancy. Aristotle, the Greek philosopher, wrote the first-ever book on reproduction, and although much of it proved to be completely unfounded (he believed that only men were responsible for conception, for example) it is nevertheless a serious attempt to understand sex.

introduction

In Ancient Rome regular sex was thought to be necessary to keep healthy. The Romans had a very liberal attitude to sex and celebrated it in art and literature, as did the Indians and Chinese. The *Kama Sutra* is one of the most famous texts about sex. Written in the second century A.D. by an Indian nobleman named Vatsyayana, it is a detailed account of the art and technique of Indian erotics and includes instructions for men on how they can best please their partner. There is also a more advanced version called the *Ananga Ranga*.

The Chinese regarded sex as very important to human health and longevity. As a result they were quite open about it and thus able to study sexual relations with an open mind for thousands of years. Its presence in everyday life is illustrated by two erotic books, *The Golden Lotus* and *The Love of the Emperor and the Japanese Shunga*, which were familiar to most households. Chinese erotic art is well known; they also compiled beautifully illustrated sex manuals detailing positions with exotic names such as "leaping white tiger." Furthermore, they invented a form of erotic exercise—a type of sexual yoga—that builds up and stores *qi* (energy) and promotes good health and longevity.

Judeo-Christian and Islamic teachings were more restrictive, however. Penalties for adultery were severe, and the patriarchal society of Western culture viewed women as weaker and subordinate. Moreover, a woman was regarded as a potential temptress, who could overpower a man's sense of superiority by enticing him with her body. The body was therefore bound up with notions of sin and shame, and sexual desire became something to feel guilty about. We have still not managed to break free of this even today.

The reproductive system still fascinated inquiring minds, however. There are several beautifully illustrated anatomical books dating back to medieval times, and Leonardo Da Vinci's drawings are well known. The English physician William Harvey (1578–1657), discoverer of the circulation of the blood, at last recognized a woman's role in conception. In his *Essays on Generation in Animals*, he confirmed the doctrine that every living being has its origin in an egg. In contrast to such groundbreaking research, were writings that perpetuated the myth that normal sexual activity was unhealthy. Dr. John Harvey Kellogg (of cornflakes fame) wrote that masturbation caused acne, bed-wetting, nail-biting, and shyness. Sex continued to be seen as dangerous to the stability of society, and masturbation an act that led to insanity.

In 1867 the American temperance campaigner Elizabeth Willard (1839–98) expressed her disapproval of sex in her book *Sexology as the Philosophy of Life*. She described sex as an undignified and disgusting act that would cause disease, inflammation, and the breakdown of social order. She was particularly horrified to relate that one orgasm used up the energy needed for a full working day!

Modern times

In the late nineteenth and twentieth centuries, scientific study of sex increased. Most famously, Sigmund Freud devised a whole system of psychoanalysis based on sexuality, which we still refer to today. One of Freud's ideas was that the libido was psychosexual energy present in everyone from birth. He claimed that all psychiatric illness originated in misdirected or frustrated sexuality.

Another pioneer in the study of sexuality was English physician Henry Havelock Ellis (1859–1939), whose work changed public perceptions of

An eighteenth-century watercolor on silk from a private collection of Chinese artworks.

introduction

women's sexuality. In his book "Man and Woman" he stated that women experienced as much sexual desire and pleasure in the sex act as men, possibly more. He also believed that masturbation was a natural act and that homosexuality should not be viewed as an illness. At last!

Magnus Hirschfeld (1868–1935) also made a big impact in the field of sexual research, conducting surveys and publishing journals. In his book "Sexual Pathology" he examined the role of hormones in sexual function. This was a crucial step forward, and hormone research remains a vital part of scientific investigation today. Hirschfeld conducted research into female sexual behavior, held contraception and marriage guidance clinics, and even staged international conferences on sexual science.

In the first half of the twentieth century, sex reappeared in the public arena, and interest in contraception and sex education increased. However, it wasn't until the contraceptive pill became available in the 1960s that women truly became sexually liberated: for the first time sex could be enjoyed without risk of pregnancy. This dramatically changed sexual behavior, as did "safer sex" in the 1980s.

Since then sex has become increasingly dominant in the media— most films for adults, for example, have a sexual content of some sort. Although this has been very liberating in a number of ways it has also been the cause of many new problems. Both men and women feel they ought to be having sex as they see it in the movies, with bodies to match, or that they should be reading the "sex tips" advertised on the covers of glossy magazines, and are thus made to worry that perhaps their performance is not as good as it should be. Inadequacy is only one problem; the cultural prominence of sex can cause dissatisfaction in a relationship, or sexual addiction in one form or another.

The West has a lot to learn, and to unlearn. Its best hope is to look to the ancient teachings of other cultures, whose attitude toward sex has been so much healthier than its own.

Using sexual imagery to promote a product on a huge billboard in New York City.

About me

People have always described me as a vibrant person, full of energy, drive, ambition, and passion. Part of this passion I manifest through my libido—and it is something that, as a woman, I am proud of. I hope that by writing this book I can help others, both men and women, to achieve this, too.

I am married with children, and therefore know how hard it can be to keep the spark alive while still being true to yourself. The good news is, however, that there are many new avenues to explore and many techniques to try, and I urge you to experiment with as many as possible until you find what is right for you. For me, dancing Five Rhythms and Biodanza has proved an amazing exploration of sexual energy... I hope you, too, will find something special that ignites your passion again.

I have written this book to help people who are worried that passion in their relationship and sex life is waning. The book is about increasing the libido—increasing your desire for sex. It is designed to help people whose sex drive is depressed or nonexistent. It is NOT for people who already have a healthy libido but who just want to have more sex. I hope the book will help you enjoy lovemaking with your partner, ensuring that it is a physical, spiritual, intimate, and ultimately totally fulfilling experience.

GOOD LUCK ... RELAX ... AND HAVE FUN. Aliza Baron Cohen

CHAPTER ONE

about the libido

what is the libido?

"The sexual drive. The term is often used to refer to the intensity of sexual desires. In psycho-analytic theory the libido (like the death instinct) is one of the fundamental sources of energy for all mental life. The normal course of development can be altered by fixation at one level and by regression."

Oxford Concise Medical Dictionary

Your sex drive is controlled by many factors, such as hormones (sex hormones, metabolic hormones, brain neurotransmitters, pheromones), psychological stimuli (such as imagination, mood, and sight), physical stimuli (such as taste, smell, and touch) and cultural customs. People often find that as they grow older their sex drive begins to decline, and this is because the body produces fewer sex hormones as we age.

A low libido— does it matter?

Having a good sex drive has a big effect on your overall health. Increased sexual vitality is beneficial for mind, body, and soul. Many studies have found that both men and women are generally healthier and much less prone to disease if they have sex regularly.

Women

- Sex at least once a week helps to regulate the menstrual cycle, reduces PMS, and increases fertility.
- Abstinence lowers a woman's oestrogen levels. Low estrogen is linked to the onset of menopausal and menstrual problems.
- Studies have shown that menopausal women having regular sex experience fewer hot flashes and age more slowly than those who have sex less than once a week.
- Having sex on a regular basis has also been found to be good for toning the pelvic floor muscles, lower back, stomach, and bottom. Now, there's an incentive if ever I've heard one!

Men and women—how different are we?

Communicating our needs

Women are often embarrassed to talk to their partner about their sexual relationship, and very few women are openly proud of their desire. Pressures of work and family responsibilities seem to consume a woman's energy and thoughts, making sex less of an priority. Men, on the other hand, tend to boast about how much they think about or want sex, yet are not so forthcoming when they need help for a sexual problem. Sadly, when men think about boosting their libido, they usually believe this means increasing the frequency and size of their erections and improving their sexual performance.

Sexual peak

Women are supposed to reach the peak of their sex drive in their thirties or forties, but for men it happens during their teens.

Men

- Testosterone levels increase during and after sex, which may help to protect men from osteoporosis and heart disease.
- Regular sex is thought to help prevent congestion and inflammation of the prostate gland.
- After sex, men produce a high level of the hormone oxytocin (see page 23)—in fact, much more than women do—which helps them to feel relaxed and sleep well. This is why men sleep straight after sex, whereas women are ready to snuggle up and talk or go for round two!
- Regular sex can also make a man feel more committed to the relationship, because oxytocin is also the hormone that makes people feel "in love."
- Sexual prowess is believed to be inextricably bound up with a man's self-image, so that men who struggle with low libido can find all aspects of their life affected.

hormones

Hormones are chemical messengers that pass information around the body. Each messenger is dependent on the next, and if one is out of balance it affects all the others. Hormones are produced in the body and are transported by the blood. Sex hormones are vital for healthy sexual function in both men and women. There are many different hormones that affect the libido, while fluctuating hormone levels can cause women's sexual drive— as well as moods and emotions—to vary throughout their menstrual cycle, pregnancy, and menopause.

Everything that lowers the libido (see page 28) also has an effect on the hormone levels. Some of these things can depress your fertility as well as your libido. Exercise that is too vigorous, or saunas or baths that are too hot are good examples, as they can reduce the production of male hormones and thus affect the quality and amount of the sperm.

Sex drive is influenced mainly by the hormones testosterone, estrogen, and progesterone, but there are other hormones that also affect the body's sexual functioning. Below is a list of the hormones and the role they play in helping us to maintain a healthy libido.

When we fall in love, hormones, neurotransmitters and other body chemicals trigger intense physical feelings. This is what happens in your body when you meet someone, find them attractive, begin a relationship, fall in love, and then commit to a long-term relationship. **Pheromones**, secreted by men and women, boost attraction. **Adrenaline** fires up the energy for the desire, and the heart starts to beat faster. **Dopamine** levels increase to intensify sexual feelings. **Testosterone** and **estrogen** (and other hormones) charge the libido. **PEA** triggers the love-struck, giddy sensation and orgasm enjoyment. **Oxytocin** helps a couple to bond and develop an attachment.

ANDROSTENEDIONE

Androstenedione is a male hormone, produced by both men and women, that helps increase the production of testosterone. It enhances the libido almost immediately.

DHEA

DHEA (dehydroepiandosterone) is an androgen that converts to androstenedione and increases sexual desire. It raises testosterone levels and is often described as the master sex hormone. It is made in huge quantities during puberty and reaches a peak during your early twenties, when it starts to drop. High levels of DHEA are linked with a healthy sex drive.

Exercise can increase DHEA levels, but it needs to be rigorous exercise, for 30 minutes a day for one month, before you will see any results (but don't overdo it, since too much exercise can actually impede sex drive). DHEA levels can also be increased with stress-reduction techniques and dietary adjustments. It is also thought to be a good anti-aging nutrient, which boosts energy levels, improves sex drive, aids sleep, lifts the mood, and reduces stress.

But before you run out to buy truck-loads of DHEA, you should know that too much of this hormone can stimulate the growth of facial hair in women and can cause acne, insomnia and irritability in either sex. That's enough to put anyone off!

Sexual addiction

It would be irresponsible to write a book like this without touching upon the dangers of sexual activity when it is used in the wrong way.

Sexuality can generate passion, love, romance, pleasure, and desire, but it can also act as a destructive and negative force, which lies behind many of today's social problems, causing dissatisfaction, destruction, pain, and unhappiness. At its most extreme, it can result in sexual addiction, rape, sexual abuse, perversion, and violence.

How do you know if you are an addict or if you have a problem?

Just like drugs, alcohol, or gambling, sex can be addictive. Whether it be sex with strangers, masturbation, or Internet porn, as with all other addictions the compulsions are pursued in secret, with enormous cost to the individual, their career, their family, and their friends. If you are prepared to risk sacrificing all this to feed your desire, you have a very real problem.

The term "sex addict" is very broad and can encompass every type of sexual activity, but the problem is little known about and it is not something that people talk about. Whereas alcoholics, drug addicts, and gamblers can be open about their problem and will receive sympathetic support to help them break their habit, sex addicts find it very hard to talk about their continuous craving for sexual excitement.

Just as in other kinds of addiction, sex addicts experience a high. It is thought that about 10 percent of Americans are sex addicts. Their inability to control their behavior, fear of discovery, self-disgust, and guilt felt at putting their loved ones at risk merely increases their desire to escape once more into their addiction. Such behavior has been recognized as a problem only within the last two decades.

If you think you or anyone you know is suffering from a sex addiction, there is help out there. See page 140 for more information.

DOPAMINE

Dopamine is the chemical that makes an activity pleasurable. It causes you to feel excited, enthusiastic, happy, boosts sex drive, and makes orgasm easier to achieve. When levels of dopamine increase and are released into the bloodstream, sexual feelings become intensified. Low levels weaken sex drive because of its role in the production of testosterone. Dopamine levels can be increased with exercise and by eating a balanced diet, but are easily depleted through stress.

ESTROGEN

Estrogen is, in fact, not one but a group of hormones that play an important role in the female libido, and is secreted mainly by the ovaries. Levels fluctuate throughout the monthly cycle and tend to decrease as women age. Estrogen has many important functions, including keeping the vagina lubricated, so that sex is pleasurable. When oestrogen levels fall (around the time of the menopause, for example) sex can become painful, so the prospect of sex can lose its appeal. Smaller quantities of estrogen are secreted in men, and when it is given as a supplement (normally to treat prostate cancer) it often has the side effect of increasing their libido, too.

FSH

FSH (follicle-stimulating hormone) is essential for healthy sexual functioning. It is needed in women for the production and release of eggs and in men for sperm production.

LH

LH (luteinizing hormone) influences the production of progesterone in women and also stimulates testosterone production in men.

OXYTOCIN

Oxytocin is a hormone secreted by the pituitary gland. It helps with the contraction of muscles in the penis, vagina, and uterus during orgasm. It is also involved in milk letdown during breast feeding. It is the hormone that makes you feel that you are in love, and therefore keeps you persistent during the early stages of a relationship; it also brings on drowsiness and so helps you to have a good night's sleep after sex. Its levels rise whenever you think of someone you find attractive, and increase still more if you are close to them or are having sex.

PEA

PEA (phenylethylamine) is a chemical produced in the body that causes the sensations you associate with falling in love. You may feel giddy and euphoric, as if you are walking on air, often with a churning feeling in your stomach, or you lose your appetite and notice an increase in your heart rate. The euphoric state it creates helps to raise the libido. Unfortunately, once you have begun a relationship, PEA can start to decrease as early as six months later. This is when the next stage of the relationship should start, as the chemical oxytocin is then thought to generate feelings of attachment. PEA is also released during orgasm to strengthen the

Chemical copies of human pheremones can be put into perfumes and aftershaves (without affecting the smell), or into candles.

sensation. Some believe that it is mildly addictive (which accounts for the chocoholics among us, since PEA is released when you eat chocolate, and may contribute to some people's addiction to sex—see page 22). PEA is also released when you exercise.

PHEROMONES

The word "pheromone" is derived from the Greek "*pherein,*" meaning "to bring to," and "*hormon,*" meaning "to excite." So, not surprisingly, pheromones are the chemicals that our bodies make to excite us and entice the opposite sex. We secrete them when we see someone we find attractive, and when that person picks up the smell, they release pheromones of their own. Pheromones also give indications of our emotional state, our physical strength, and our sexual status. They are supposed to have a musty smell, a little like sandalwood, and are secreted by glands in the lips, around the mouth, armpits, eyelids, genitals, nipples, and outer ears. Women are more aware of pheromones than men. Fifty percent of people can't smell them, but the very presence of pheromones is perceived subliminally and affects many of our sex hormones.

The most powerful pheromone is thought to be androstenone, made in the body from testosterone. It is the primary male pheromone instinctively produced by men to attract women. Deodorants can inhibit its release, since they block the pores. Pheromones are thought to be so sexually potent that some perfume manufacturers now add pheromones to their products in the hope that their effects will increase sales.

PROGESTERONE

Often known as the "happy mood hormone," progesterone is produced in both men and women. The word has a Latin derivation, literally meaning "preceding gestation," or "before pregnancy." It plays an important role in preparing the body for pregnancy. Men, however, also need enough progesterone for the production of testosterone—low levels can cause an increase in prolactin (a hormone produced by the pituitary gland), which can cause erection problems. You can increase your body's progesterone production through vitamin and herbal supplements (see page 49) or herbal creams, such as Mexican yam.

PROSTAGLANDINS

Not hormones, but hormonelike substances, prostaglandins are fatty acids important for the contraction of smooth muscles, which makes sex more enjoyable.

SEROTONIN

Serotonin is present in the brain, intestines, and blood platelets, and acts as a neurotransmitter, as well as inducing vasoconstriction and contraction of the smooth muscles. It affects your need for food and sex, and too much can depress the appetite, decrease your libido, and make it harder to achieve an orgasm, although it is a relaxant. Low levels of serotonin can cause depression and aggressive behavior. Carbohydrates stimulate the production of serotonin, while weight loss reduces it and boosts your sex drive.

TESTOSTERONE

Testosterone is known as the male hormone, but it is also secreted in women and has an effect on their libido as well—it is the main hormone responsible for lust in both men and women. Testosterone is produced in the testes, ovaries, and adrenal glands. It has often been thought that girls who were tomboys before puberty had high levels of testosterone and would go on to develop a high sex drive as they matured. Testosterone is linked with genital development, libido, sexual sensitivity, and intensity of orgasm. Boys experience a surge of testosterone in puberty, which makes them very sexually driven; it also dramatically changes their behavior. For most men, libido peaks from 18 years onward and then very gradually declines. Testosterone levels also slowly begin to decrease. Young men with a low sex drive, little body hair, and a tendency to tire easily are probably low in testosterone.

This understanding of testosterone has led to testosterone replacement therapy, but this will not make men with an already healthy libido increase their sex drive still further or achieve a stronger erection. As long as there is a continuous supply of testosterone available to brain cells, the libido, sexual performance and satisfaction will be fine. Testosterone becomes less available as men age, however; and therefore the libido decreases, but there are effective natural ways in which men can boost production.

chakras and their influence on the libido

Many Eastern practices, including Tantra, are based on the belief that energy flows through invisible "channels" within the body known as chakras, and from person to person. In terms of Western medicine, these chakras correspond to the endocrine system, which controls hormone secretion and keeps the body balanced. It is vital that the chakras remain in harmony with each other, and therefore you need to know which chakra needs attention at any given time.

There are many different ways of looking at the chakras, and they can tell you many different things about your life and emotional state. A good healer can try to determine why you are feeling physically or emotionally out of balance according to the energy of your chakras, and can help harmonize them once more. It is a vast subject, which you may like to study in more depth (see page 141 for suggested reading). Here I have listed the chakras that can tell you about your libido and your sexual energy.

You need to maintain a healthy balance in both the hormonal and chakral systems if you are to enjoy a healthy sex drive. If you suspect that you may have an imbalance, read on....

The crown chakra

This chakra is all about spiritual connection. When it is open, sex can become a universal magical experience. If it is closed, however, it can become just about the self in the present moment.

The third eye

If this chakra is closed, it can lead to an over-dependence on others, since you feel unable to see clearly yourself—it is a little like being blind. This is also the chakra involved in intuition.

The throat chakra

The throat chakra is all about communication, so if it is open you can communicate your desires and the things you enjoy. If it is closed you feel unable to say if you don't like something—perhaps that sex is not as you would like it to be!

The heart chakra

The heart chakra is associated with altruistic love and the ability to surrender. If this chakra is open, you feel as if you are in love. When it is closed, you feel cut off, closed, scared of getting hurt and unable to love. You feel vulnerable or afraid of commitment.

The solar plexus chakra

This is the chakra that is most connected with personal identity. It is also the chakra associated with love. When it is blocked, sex can feel threatening. The person may feel as if it's difficult to let go or to receive any love.

The sacral chakra

This chakra is the creative and sexual center. It governs pleasure, fertility, and desire. If energy flows smoothly here, you feel full of life. If the energy is blocked, the sexual energy will be stifled or reduced, and you can feel stiff in the lower back. People may be reluctant to have sex, or if they do it will feel functional, rather than an emotional or sensual experience.

The base chakra

The base chakra lies at the base of the spine and is where the sleeping Kundalini energy can be found (see page 107). When your energy flows smoothly in this chakra, your sex life feels grounded, without fear, and complete.

loss of libido: causes and effects

Has sex become an effort? Has the spark gone out of your love life? Is it easier just to go to sleep than try to arouse your partner? Do you sometimes think you'd rather have a nice cup of milky hot chocolate? If the answer to any of these questions is yes, one of you is probably suffering from a low libido, and your love life is in definite need of a boost.

The problem is very common—affecting around a fifth of the population—and the feelings of sadness, anger, frustration, loneliness, and rejection it can serve only to make matters worse. Many couples resign themselves to the situation, considering it an inevitability in a long-term relationship, or blame themselves for their partner's loss of interest, thinking themselves unattractive or at fault in some way. Sadly, people are generally unaware that this is not the case, and that help is at hand.

This book shows you not only how to work on your own libido but how to help your partner as well. There are many things you can do together to re-ignite the spark, as well as treatments, techniques, exercises, and disciplines you can try to help you become intimate again. Almost everybody will see results within just a few weeks of using self-help techniques such as vitamins, herbs, tonics, massage, essential oils, and exercise.

It's important to bear in mind that a low libido can be a reflection of your general health, lifestyle, and stress levels as well as the state of your relationship. If you are constantly lacking in energy, under a lot of pressure, or suffering from regular aches and pains, then eventually your libido will be affected. Take care of your health, and try to make changes to your lifestyle, and it's more than likely you will see a big difference in your libido.

ALCOHOL

Most people regard alcohol as an aphrodisiac. True, it can certainly instill some Dutch courage, relax you, and make you less inhibited; however, as Shakespeare put it, even though it increases desire, it also "takes away the performance."

Alcohol can function as an aphrodisiac, but only when imbibed in small quantities, and then mainly for women, since it makes their testosterone levels rise. However, it does not do this for men—any amount of alcohol interferes with testosterone production, lowering sperm count, and sex drive. So sorry, boys, all it gives you is the courage!

After a few drinks, alcohol starts to hamper a man's performance, inhibiting an erection. Large quantities of alcohol can also impede a woman's libido, since it lowers estrogen levels. Excessive amounts can cause fertility and menstrual problems, and impotence in men.

Alcohol also can decrease penis size and shrink the testicles—and if that prospect doesn't stop a man from getting plastered, nothing will! The good news is that if you stop drinking, sex drive and fertility in both men and women can improve within three months.

Common causes of a fall in libido

Stress • depression • anxiety • low self-esteem • poor body image • tiredness and lack of sleep • menopause (both male and female) • under-active ovaries/testicles • hormone deficiencies • prostate problems • hysterectomy • previous sexual abuse • relationship difficulties • smoking • drugs and alcohol • poor diet • lack of exercise • obesity • familiarity • low sunlight exposure • having a baby • breast-feeding • very hot baths and saunas

SMOKING

Smoking depresses the libido—and unless your partner smokes too, the smell of your stale, smoky breath will certainly depress theirs!

Cigarettes affect men and women in different ways. They can lower a woman's estrogen levels and even bring on the menopause two to three years early. They lower testosterone levels in men, and the effect of nicotine on the circulation can result in erectile dysfunction as the blood supply to the penis is affected. Just two cigarettes smoked before sex will markedly decrease the flow of blood.

People who cut down their smoking or stop altogether can significantly increase their sex drive. But don't get impatient: it takes between four and eight weeks before the benefits become apparent, by which time the sperm count is said to have increased significantly and erections become more rigid.

SUGAR and REFINED CARBOHYDRATES

Sugar and refined carbohydrates (such as those found in cakes, cookies, and other sweets) can also lower your libido, since they affect blood sugar levels and deplete chromium and B complex vitamins (see pages 48 and 51). This will drain your energy, making you feel too tired for sex, but can also affect your enjoyment and drive, since these vitamins are important for circulation and hormone production.

How is it affecting your relationship?

Having a low sex drive can affect your relationship, your happiness, and your life. You might find that your partner becomes insecure and worried that something is wrong between you, especially if your libido used to be high. Often people feel under pressure to have sex in order to reassure their partner that nothing is wrong, and this pressure can itself also be a cause in lowering libido.

CAFFEINE

Caffeine is present in coffee, tea, cola, and other carbonated drinks. It depletes the body of zinc, magnesium, manganese, and other nutrients important for sexual health (see pages 47—51).

DRUGS

Both prescription and illegal drugs can affect your sex drive. These include heart and blood pressure pills, diuretics, tranquillizers, antidepressants, steroids, some antihistamines, oral contraceptives, cancer treatments, and opiates.

If you think your sex drive has dipped since you started a certain medication, speak to your doctor, so that he/she can adjust the dosage or perhaps prescribe something else. Do not stop taking your medication without the supervision of your doctor.

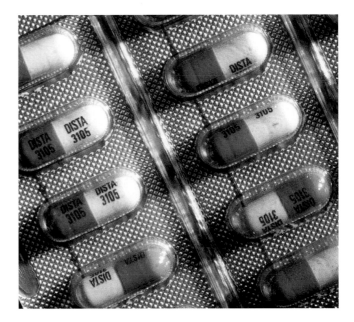

HORMONE DISRUPTORS

Most people have never heard of hormone disruptors, but they are ubiquitous in the developed world— they can be found in pollutants, drugs, meat and fish, plastic, and pesticides—and it is almost impossible to avoid them. Crucially, they affect reproductive health—they interfere with the whole endocrine system and the communication of glands, hormones, and cells in your body. They play havoc with your sexuality, too. Foods sprayed with pesticides are especially bad, since they contain hormonelike substances such as exogenous estrogens and androgens (the male and female hormones)

which are very damaging to your sexual health—they break down your own hormones and create an imbalance. The major fluctuations in hormonal levels they can cause are harmful to your libido, fertility, energy, and general health. It is best to eat organic food where possible, especially meats and dairy products, which are otherwise notoriously high in hormone-disrupting chemicals.

LACK OF SLEEP

No one feels like having sex when they are tired and irritable from lack of sleep. Many people experience insomnia and broken nights, especially if they have young children—in fact, sleep problems affect a third of the population. Nevertheless, sleep is vital for good health and performance.

How do you know if you have a low libido?

Everyone's sex drive is different, and our libido adapts to different circumstances throughout our lives. It is best not to compare your drive with someone else's as everyone's definition of even a low sex drive will be different. For some people a low sex drive means wanting sex once a week, while for others it's once every two weeks—or not even that.

People who suffer from a very low libido often don't think about sex very much, nor do they have erotic fantasies and dreams or any desire to have sex or masturbate. If you've noticed that your desire for sex used to be higher—or has completely diminished—then you need to address the problem.

STRESS

Stress is a well-known libido-killer! This is because it triggers the release of adrenaline (epinephrine), large quantities of which make you unable to relax. In fact it prepares the body for fight or flight, boosting circulation in the limbs, for example, at the expense of the parts of the body that aren't needed, such as the genitals. Stress also reduces DHEA levels (see page 21), and estrogen and testosterone levels fall as well. Sex drive can be affected by many emotions and states of mind connected with stress. If people become anxious, angry, or depressed, they produce chemicals that can interfere with their sexual response.

ANXIETY When men feel anxious, they find it difficult to control their arousal and can climax too quickly, whereas women unconsciously block out their sexual excitement.

DANGER The physiological states brought about by anger and sexual arousal are very similar, and a little anger can actually make people very sexually responsive. Those who repress their anger may also be holding back their sexual expression, and therefore managing your anger may help you to enjoy sex more. At the other end of the scale, too much anger will turn off sexual desire completely.

DEPRESSION When we are depressed, our testosterone levels decrease, resulting in a loss of sexual desire and drive. Depression can manifest itself in many forms, such as low self-confidence and self-esteem and poor body image—all of which make you less likely to want and enjoy sex when you value yourself so little.

Sex isn't pleasant when you are stressed, so it is very important to learn how to relax properly. For some basic things you can do yourself to reduce your stress levels, read on.

Don't be afraid to talk about it

In many cases, loss of libido is attributable to psychological and emotional difficulties. Problems arising from relationships, insecurity, and conflicting emotions, abuse (sexual, physical, or psychological), worry, fatigue, overwork, and financial concerns are just a few among many common causes. Sexual problems themselves frequently remain unaddressed and prevent you from enjoying a healthy sex life. Family therapists, relationship counselors, and marriage and sex therapists can all help, as can most forms of psychotherapy and counseling.

CHAPTER TWO

therapies

and

treatments

rediscovering desire

Many people want to know what they can do or take to increase their libido—especially men (who often think this will improve their sexual performance, make their erections last longer, or turn their partner into a sex goddess!). Nowadays many couples will automatically think about Viagra and hormone treatments (see pages 134–5), but these can have dangerous side effects.

It is often more beneficial to seek the advice of a health practitioner than self-prescribing, whatever your condition. Loss of libido is no exception, and even though it may at first seem embarrassing to talk about, remember that your health practitioner has heard it all a thousand times before.

If you increase your libido the natural way, you will not only rekindle your desire, but will also improve your physical, emotional, and spiritual health. It's easy and it's enjoyable, and it may be one of the most important things you ever do.

Boosting your libido the natural way

Before you do anything else, it is important to have a checkup with your doctor to make sure there are no medical conditions that have affected your sex drive or caused erectile dysfunction. Once you've

Simple lifestyle changes

You may be surprised how quickly you notice an improvement when you try the following. But if you see no benefit after three months, consult a health practitioner for more personalized advice.

- Eat a healthy, balanced diet that is low in animal fats, fried food, sugar, white flour, and junk food.
- Avoid harmful substances, such as drugs.
- Boost your nitric oxide levels (see page 53) to improve circulation, especially to the genitals.
- Try the recommended herbal supplements and tonics.
- Take vitamin and mineral supplements, as deficiencies can cause a low libido.
- Practice confidence-building exercises and stress-reduction activities, such as deep-breathing exercises, visualizations, and meditation.
- Take more exercise, since sexual energy can be increased by yoga and regular aerobic activity.
- Discover new ways to spice up your relationship and develop more intimacy together through massage and tantric exercises.
- Try some alternative treatments (preferably with a practitioner) or, if you're feeling a little daunted by the prospect, at least experiment with some of the more basic self-help methods, such as acupressure, homeopathy, aromatherapy, and using flower essences.

established that your problem is not directly health related, you can learn about the many and varied natural remedies and techniques there are to choose from, and decide which will work best for you.

This chapter examines the most effective ways to increase your sex drive naturally, looking at changes in lifestyle and alternative treatments you can try at home or pursue with the help of a practitioner. Perhaps just a reassessment of diet, exercise routine and relaxation will do the trick. Before we go into detail, take a look at the box above for an at-a-glance view of the things you could try.

exercise

Exercise is a great tonic for the libido. Apart from the obvious physical benefits, it makes you feel very good about yourself and your body. And once you feel good about your body, you'll feel more inclined to show it.

To say that this is a vital thing during sex may seem to be stating the obvious, but the importance of physical self-confidence cannot be overemphasized. Many people who lose weight find that their lovemaking acquires a new lease on life: when they were overweight they felt very negative about themselves and uncomfortable and vulnerable when they took their clothes off.

Furthermore, exercise is fantastic for your heart and circulation, which again are vital for a good libido. Don't be impatient—you won't see the benefits overnight, but you will with a little time and effort. Exercise also promotes deep relaxation, which is important because stress lowers levels of sex hormones and sexual desire.

Activities that combine physical exercise with controlled breathing (such as yoga and t'ai chi) are the best, since they approximate a moving meditation that increases energy flow and shifts energy blocks. It is this that gives us heightened sensitivity when making love.

If you prefer to stick just to your usual exercise

routine (perhaps running, boxing, or cycling), all you have to do is to add a more meditative element to it. For example, imagine or visualize energy flowing around your body, count as you run or walk, or even just say "left, right, left, right" (which in itself can be very relaxing) and focus on your breathing.

Making love is itself an important form of exercise. It increases the supply of oxygen to the cells, releases endorphins, and lowers cholesterol. It also balances the hormones and plays a major role in their production. Sex increases estrogen production, especially in menopausal women, and boosts testosterone levels in men and women. It also regulates the menstrual cycle and increases the production of adrenal hormones.

Aerobic exercise—such as dancing, walking, tennis, swimming, and running—is good for your overall health as well as your sexual health. Aim for about 20–45 minutes a day. It will do wonders for your self-image, and before long you will begin to enjoy the new, toned you with your partner. A positive self-image is one of the key requisites for a happy sex life.

There are some types of exercise that are specifically geared toward awakening your sexual energy. These include some forms of dance, such as Biodanza and Five Rhythms, some yoga positions, and "sexercises," also known as Kegels (see pages 41–2). For more advanced techniques, see the chapter on tantric and Taoist healing (page 105).

Dance

Dance is one of the sexiest forms of exercise. It has been used as a seduction technique for many

Exercise has a direct effect on our libido, since it balances the hormonal system and releases endorphins, which are feel-good chemicals well known for affecting our sex drive and sexual health. According to research, people who exercise regularly tend to have more sex, and experience better and more satisfying orgasms than those who live more sedentary lives. Women get aroused more quickly, and men achieve stronger erections.

thousands of years and provides a means for couples to see how well their bodies move together. Dancing also enables you to let go of the stress and worries of the day in a really enjoyable way that doesn't feel like exercise. There are many different types of dancing that you can try; some are very structured, but with others you can do as you please.

In my experience the best types of dancing for the purpose of enhancing your libido are Five Rhythms and Biodanza (you may be able to find classes near you by looking on the Internet). Five Rhythms is a freestyle dance to music of various types, in which you work through five rhythms/emotions as you dance. It is a dance without ego that has nothing to do with the latest style or fashionable steps. It is a very liberating experience that frees your soul as well as your sexual energy and rids you of your hang-ups.

Biodanza is similar but has much more structure, and the music often has a South American feel. The concept is still the same: to free your body of unwanted emotions and patterns of behavior while also unlocking your energy (especially your sexual and creative energy).

If you can't get to a class, try to do some dancing at home. Be playful. Put on your favorite music, some fast and some slow. Gradually let your body move to the rhythm, forgetting whether what you are doing looks good or right. Let go of the tension in your body bit by bit. Let go of your shoulders, neck, back, hips, knees, elbows, wrists, and jaw, and allow the music to take you on a journey. Flow with the rhythms, and remember to breathe.

It is also good to dance with your partner in this way; try to maintain eye contact and touch each other in a sensual way while dancing. Don't be critical of your partner's dancing, just try to see them for who they are—your lover. You should feel quite sexual and sensual after this, and very relaxed—often people find themselves laughing together. It is important to focus on releasing the hips, as this is where sexual energy can become very stuck.

Pelvic exercises

Some types of exercise can help you strengthen the muscles you use in sex—your pubococcygeus (PC muscle), or pelvic floor—and increase your libido by making you aware of the sexual energy as it flows in your pelvis and genitals. Some of these exercises can also help to delay ejaculation (and prevent urinary incontinence). They have been used for centuries in many different cultures and ancient traditions to invigorate the genitals.

PELVIC LIFTS

These help to keep the pelvis toned and flexible and promote the flow of blood to the genitals, releasing sexual energy and boosting desire. Do not do pelvic lifts if you have back problems.

Lie on your back with your knees bent, your feet flat on the bed or floor, and your arms by your side with your palms facing downward. Lift the pelvis as high as you can, and breathe deeply. Hold each lift for about 10 seconds and do as many as you can.

PELVIC CIRCLING

Many cultures outside the Western world believe that it is normal to allow the hips to move freely. You can see this in the way they dance and walk. Westerners tend to be much stiffer around this area, and it is very important to loosen the hips in order to unlock any sexual repression or hang-ups and free up sexual energy. Moving your hips also increases circulation to the genitals and glands.

Stand with your feet hip-width apart, and move your hips in small circles. Move as smoothly as possible, and gradually make the circles bigger, as if you're playing with a hula hoop (you can try this with your partner if it helps). Move your hips first in one direction and then in the other. Do several repetitions on each side.

KEGEL EXERCISES FOR WOMEN

Kegels are also known as pelvic floor exercises. They were originally designed to stop incontinence, but an added bonus is that they tone the vagina, enhancing sexual sensation and enabling it to hold the penis tightly during sex. Imagine trying to stop yourself from urinating—the muscles you contract are the

Reducing stress and finding sexual energy

Feeling tired or stressed can dampen your sexual drive, so it is important to find effective ways to unwind and get your sexual energy flowing again.

Besides exercise, you can try a whole range of complementary remedies. Taking time out for yourself by having leisurely walks and aromatherapy baths, having a massage, writing a journal, or calling a friend will all ease the problem.

To strengthen your pelvic floor, tense your muscles as if you were trying to stop yourself from urinating.

Tense them as much as you can, and hold for 10 seconds. Then let go. Repeat 12 times and at intervals throughout the day.

PELVIC FLOOR TOGETHER

During your lovemaking sessions, spend a minute practicing your Kegel exercises. The woman can try to squeeze her partner's penis tightly, using only the muscles around her vagina. Hold for a few seconds, then release, and repeat a couple of times.

Then the man can flex his penis, making it move toward the upper wall of her vagina: holding, releasing, and repeating.

Apart from its enormous benefits for your sex life and your bladder, this exercise feels good, too!

ones you use for this exercise. Contract them as tightly as you can, and then release. Repeat 10–15 times, varying the speed, and aim for several sessions during the day.

KEGELS FOR MEN

Men should also tone their pelvic floor, for when this muscle is strong it helps to maintain a firm erection. It can also help delay ejaculation and prolong intercourse.

Yoga

Yoga is now enjoying mainstream popularity in the West; it has become the fashionable way to relax, stretch, and tone; but more importantly, it is a very effective way to start feeling great.

What is less known about yoga is the effect it has on your energy levels, especially your sexual energy. Hormones are secreted just by doing yoga, as many of the postures stimulate the glands that produce them. Yoga can increase strength, endurance, and flexibility, allowing you to bend into new and exciting positions. The following two yoga postures are great for boosting the energy in the sex chakras (see page 27):

THE BUTTERFLY

This exercise opens up your hips and pelvis, which circulates energy to the genitals and increases their sensitivity. It is this area that often becomes stiff as we accumulate and retain more and more sexual problems and pain associated with past relationships, so it is very important to focus on this part of the body when you're aiming to awaken sexual energy.

- Sit on the floor with your back straight, knees apart, and the soles of your feet touching each other.
- Hold your ankles or feet; using your elbows, gently push your knees down toward the floor as far as they will go.
- Gently bounce the knees up and down.

THE INVERTED BUTTERFLY

This exercise energizes the sexual chakras (see page 27) while also opening up the heart and pelvis. It allows the energy to flow from the heart to the genitals and also improves the circulation to the genitals and chest.

- Lie on your back with your knees bent, putting your feet flat on the floor. Open your legs, pressing the soles of your feet together, and let your knees fall as far as they will go toward the floor (but don't force them down). Feel the tension in your inner thighs.
- Put your hands behind your head, and drop your elbows open to the floor. Remember to breathe, and as you breathe, relax more into the position.
- Start to become aware of your genitals, as if you were breathing into them. When you inhale, relax the area around your genitals. As you exhale, tense the pelvic floor muscles (see pages 41–2).

visualization and meditation

It is difficult to remember pleasurable feelings, just as it is difficult to remember how pain feels. People with a low libido therefore have little to motivate them to try to experience sex again. Using visualizations and scents can help you to memorize pleasurable feelings.

To boost your sex drive, burn a scented candle or some aromatherapy oil when you make love, so that in future you can use the same smell to trigger the memory of sensory pleasure.

Apparently smelling your partner's unwashed clothing while thinking about sex can help to increase your libido. Personally I think this might put me off sex altogether!

Visualization

Visualization is a meditative technique that uses the power of imagination, as if you are showing yourself a film that then becomes ingrained in your consciousness. It is a tool used by sports people, who visualize winning, for example, and by people suffering from a long-term illness who visualize themselves getting better.

Erotic visualization can play an important role in increasing sexual desire. It may help to use colors and symbols, be it imagining dressing up for your lover or thinking of your lover wearing red, or picturing them in a particular item of clothing you think is especially sexy.

Another idea worth trying is to cast your mind back to the few weeks after you first met—what it felt like, what turned you on, and how you were caught in the throes of passion just by looking at them. Really conjure up the image of that initial attraction; remember the sensations in your body, make them even more powerful, and see the picture as brightly as possible. If you want music, make it as loud as possible and allow yourself to become carried away with the film you screen in your mind. This visualization will have an immediate effect when you next see your partner and you might even notice a difference in the way they behave toward you!

Meditation

Meditation is great for your general well-being and for making you feel rejuvenated, but it can also refresh your outlook on lovemaking. How? Because as well as calming and relaxing you, it also teaches you to focus your mind, so that you can then bring a state of meditative awareness into your sexual life. Then, when you are having sex, you can really focus on the sensations you are experiencing as well as on your connection with your partner, instead of allowing yourself to become distracted by the other things that are going on in your life. Learning to be more present during lovemaking means that your attention is totally absorbed by the sensations of the moment—the feel of your partner's lips, their skin, their breathing, and the energy moving between you. Sex becomes more intimate and enjoyable, while you become more in touch with your body and its sensations.

However you choose to meditate—and there are a variety of techniques—aim for 20 minutes a day, ideally at the same time each day. I think that many people believe they have to learn to meditate and that it must be something very difficult. This is untrue: all you need to do is find a quiet place where you won't be disturbed. Close your eyes and begin to focus on your breathing. As thoughts come into your head (and they will, no matter how experienced you are), gently push them away, knowing that you can think about them again in 20 minutes' time, and go back to focusing on your breathing. This is meditation—it's that simple.

diet and nutrition

It is well known these days that our choice of food is inextricably linked to our physical and mental health, but many people overlook the fact that it also affects how we make love.

The right diet can radically improve the health of our sexual organs and boost our libido. A low libido can be the direct result of a diet that is lacking in certain nutrients, whereas a good diet makes you more energetic and can transform your sex life.

The hormones that regulate your sex drive (see page 19) all need niacin (vitamin B3), vitamin B5, vitamin A (beta carotene), and zinc, for example; and opposite you will find a list of foods that contain these nutrients. If you are not eating enough of these foods, eventually your hormonal system will become unbalanced and your libido will suffer.

Also, foods that contain the amino acids L-tyrosine and L-arginine help stimulate alertness and arousal, both of which are necessary for a healthy sex drive. Proteins, therefore, are important for increasing your libido, since they are a good source of amino acids. Algae supplements, such as blue-green algae, spirulina, and chlorella, are another good source of amino acids and vitamins. They will also help to give you energy. Of course, the "right diet" is shaped as much by what we omit as by what we include. For what to avoid, see pages 29–31.

So what should we eat?

- Fruit and vegetables …since many of them can balance female hormones. This helps with PMS, menopausal symptoms, and fatigue, as well as low sex drive. They are also beneficial to men, especially for their prostate health. Remember to eat at least five portions a day.

- Foods that are rich in estrogen-like substances … especially if for some reason your estrogen levels are low (because of the menopause, for example). These include sprouts and seeds, (such as alfalfa and sesame), beans (mung beans, soy beans, and soy products); nuts (almonds, cashews, hazel nuts, peanuts, walnuts); whole grains (corn, buckwheat, millet, oats, rye, wheat); fruits (apples, avocados, bananas, mangoes, papayas, rhubarb); dried fruits (dates, figs, prunes, raisins); dark green leafy vegetables (broccoli, spinach, watercress); other vegetables (celery, fennel, Chinese leaves, kohl rabi); pulses (chickpeas, lentils), (garbanzos); and honey.

- Foods that contain essential fatty acids (EFAs) … since these have a beneficial effect on your hormonal system. These foods include seaweeds, seafood, and oily fish, nuts, and seeds (especially walnuts, hemp seed, flaxseed, and pumpkin seed). These seeds should be eaten daily, as they help the body to make hormones called prostaglandins (see page 25), which are needed for a healthy sex drive. Sunflower seeds, raw wheatgerm, soy beans, and eggs also help sexual function for the same reason. Also oils such as linseed oil and olive oil are very high in EFAs.

- Foods rich in zinc …since it is important for female fertility and essential for boys and young men as they mature sexually. Deficiency may cause a delay in puberty. Many men lack zinc because they lose it whenever they ejaculate (with each ejaculation 5mg of zinc can be lost). Zinc is also needed for sperm and testosterone production, and for sperm motility. It is therefore very important for increasing male sex drive. Adequate zinc levels are essential for hormonal activity and reproductive health. They also strengthen muscle endurance. Zinc is present in seafood (especially oysters), red meat, eggs, cheese,

leafy vegetables, nutritional yeast, raw wheatgerm, and whole grains. Low levels of B6 hamper production of sex hormones such as progesterone. Pure niacin is a fast-acting aphrodisiac; 100mg or more of it daily will release histamine (which is needed for orgasm) and dilate the blood vessels. This produces a flush that some people find uncomfortable. If you can bear the flush, it improves circulation around the pelvis and hence increases the libido. Foods rich in niacin include eggs, nutritional yeast, wheatgerm, avocados, dried figs, liver, meat, whole grain cereals, dried beans, peas, nuts, and fish. B6 and B3 can also be found in milk, yoghurt, cheese, fish, meat, nuts, and dried fruits.

- Foods that contain vitamin E …often referred to as the "sex vitamin" since it plays a key role in the manufacture and protection of sex hormones. It helps improve circulation and oxygen supply to the blood, engorging the penis and the clitoris. Deficiency is linked with a lowered sex drive and reduced fertility. Foods rich in vitamin E include oily fish, liver, unrefined, cold-pressed vegetable oils, nuts, eggs, leafy vegetables, and sweet potatoes. Oats have high levels of vitamin E and are good for testosterone production. They are also great for a healthy nervous system.

- Plenty of protein …since a lack of protein often causes the libido and energy levels to fall, and sperm count to drop.

pulses, whole grains, brown rice, and offal. Losing the ability to taste foods is an early sign that you might be zinc deficient.

- Foods that are high in vitamin B6 and niacin (vitamin B3) …as they help to regulate sex drive and improve circulation, especially to the genitals. Vitamin B6 contributes to the conversion of fatty acids to prostaglandins, which helps to increase the libido. It also plays a part in the regulation of testosterone in men. Foods rich in B6 include green

Vitamins and supplements

Some people are not able to eat as healthily as they would like. They may have allergies or dietary restrictions; cultural, religious, or ethical constraints prescribing their choice of food; jobs where good fresh food is not always available; or they may simply not like the foods they know to be good for them.

If you know that you don't eat a varied and healthful diet, supplementation is vital for your general health as well as for your libido. Most of these supplements are available in tablet or capsule form. Be sure to stick to the recommended dosage.

Here are some of the supplements that can help revive your libido; but even taking good multivitamin, B complex, zinc, algae, and EFA supplements would

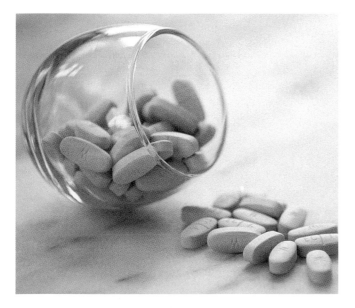

bring about a significant improvement. However, it is best to speak to a nutritionist or naturopath before you decide which to take, so that the supplements can be tailored to your individual needs.

BLUE-GREEN ALGAE

Blue-green algae (and other algae such as spirulina and chlorella) are a rich source of the vitamins, minerals and amino acids that boost your sex drive and give you more energy.

ROYAL JELLY

Royal jelly is made by bees and is rich in essential amino acids, vitamin B5, and essential fatty acids. It helps to boost energy levels and keeps you looking and feeling young, while also rejuvenating a flagging sex drive. However, don't take it on an empty stomach; and this is obviously one to be avoided if you are allergic to bee products.

BEE POLLEN

Bee pollen is the pollen that bees collect off the male parts of flowers, passing it to female parts and fertilizing them. Incorporated into the diet, it is very nourishing, since it is rich in essential fatty acids, vitamins, minerals, and amino acids. In ancient Greece bee pollen was given to people to help give them energy and increase their sex drive. It is now widely known to have beneficial effects on the libido, sexual potency, fertility, and energy. Do not take it if you are allergic to bee products.

VITAMIN A

Vitamin A is essential for the production of the sex hormones, especially estrogen and testosterone. It can be found in liver, eggs, milk, cheese, yogurt, butter, oily fish, meat, carrots, margarine, dark green leafy vegetables, and yellow-orange fruits such as peaches.

VITAMIN C

Vitamin C is very important for the health of sperm and for increasing sex drive. Vitamin C taken in supplement form also boosts semen production. It is contained in citrus fruits, strawberries, peppers, garlic, cantaloupe melons, kiwi fruit, onions, parsley, cherries, blueberries, tomatoes, potatoes, broccoli, cranberries, and cabbage.

SOYBEAN EXTRACT

Soy extracts are good for increasing a woman's estrogen levels, which can start to decrease as she grows older. They also aid the production of testosterone, which increases libido in men and women as well as stamina.

CHICKEN EGG EXTRACT

Eggs have been thought to increase sexual potency since olden days. Casanova was said to eat raw eggs when he wanted to boost his testosterone levels, but this can take between three days and three weeks to have an effect. Chicken egg extracts have been found to increase libido in men—in American trials, men taking the extracts reported a higher sex drive and a more intensive orgasm. Do not take this if you have an egg allergy.

CALCIUM

Calcium plays a big role in muscle contraction during orgasm. If you lack calcium, you may also feel irritable and tense—hardly in the mood for sex. It is found in milk, yogurt, green vegetables, canned bony fish, such as sardines, baked beans, figs, oranges, and bread.

CHROMIUM

A deficiency in chromium has been linked to a low sperm count and weakened sex drive. It can be found in wholegrain cereals, black pepper, thyme, meat, cheese, and yeast.

COPPER

Copper deficiency can result in a lowered sex drive, reduced sperm count, and even impotence. Shellfish, olives, nuts, green vegetables, whole grains, and pulses all contain copper.

IODINE

Low iodine levels can reduce sex drive and cause fatigue. Iodine can be found in seaweed, spinach, and seafood.

IRON

An iron deficiency is a common reason for people to go off sex—especially women, who can lack iron as a result of heavy periods, pregnancy, and childbirth. A lack of iron can also make you tired and listless. Iron can be found in red meat, green leafy vegetables, seafood, apricots, prunes, all dried fruit, egg yolk, watercress, wheatgerm, and wholewheat bread.

MANGANESE

Manganese deficiency is linked to a depressed sex drive and low sperm count. Manganese is found in black tea, nuts, seeds, eggs, green leafy vegetables, shellfish, dairy products, fruit, and whole grains.

MAGNESIUM

A deficiency of magnesium is linked with imbalances in sex hormones. Magnesium is vital for orgasm and sexual sensitivity.

PHOSPHORUS

Phosphorus is important for sexual arousal and semen production. It is present in dairy products, soybeans, nuts, eggs, meat, chicken, and fish.

POTASSIUM

Potassium deficiency can lower sex drive. Potassium can be found in fresh fruit and vegetables, particularly bananas.

SELENIUM

Selenium helps to block sex enzymes, and a deficiency of this element is linked with a lowered sex drive, decreased sperm count, and fertility problems. Supplementation boosts sex drive in men. Nuts—in particular Brazils—broccoli, cabbage, mushrooms, radishes, onions, garlic, celery, and seafood all contain selenium.

NITRIC OXIDE AND L-ARGININE

When the penis or clitoris is stimulated, the corpus cavernosum (a group of tiny nerves) needs to be relaxed, so that it can fill with blood during arousal. Nitric oxide is what causes this to happen. It is made by the body and is important for regulating the function of almost all the organs, including the erection of the penis.

In order to increase your levels of nitric oxide in the blood you should eat lots of nuts, such as walnuts, Brazils, almonds, cashews, and pecans. These are high in the essential amino acid L-arginine, which the body turns into nitric oxide. Other foods high in L-arginine are sesame and sunflower seeds, buckwheat, barley, coconut, gelatine, chicken, chocolate, corn, dairy products, meat, and oats.

L-arginine promotes blood flow to the penis, helping to produce harder and longer-lasting erections. It also helps to boost sex drive and sperm production. Many researchers believe that L-arginine is one of the best prosexual supplements men can take. L-arginine also helps female sex drive, since raising nitric oxide levels improves circulation in the vaginal area. It also stimulates the nerves that are involved in sexual arousal, as well as the release of growth hormone (which boosts the libido).

Do not take L-arginine if you suffer from herpes or kidney infections, as your condition will be made worse by high-arginine foods. Other amino acids that help regulate sex drive include L-phenylalanine, L-tyrosine, and L-histidine.

BORON

Boron is needed for the production of sex hormones, especially testosterone and estrogen. It can be found in fruit and vegetables.

FOLIC ACID

Folic acid maintains correct levels of the amino acid homocysteine, which has an effect on the production of nitric oxide (see left). Folic acid is found in meats, leafy green vegetables, nuts, whole grains, and brewer's yeast.

CHOLINE

The combination of choline, vitamin B5 and L-arginine is needed for nitric oxide production.

DID YOU KNOW..?
A cup of warm milk with a pinch of saffron is believed to act as an aphrodisiac for both sexes; it also increases sperm count.

acupressure and acupuncture

Acupressure is the massaging of pressure points to help clear blockages in the meridians. It also helps stimulate circulation of *qi*, blood, and bodily fluids and is thus beneficial for sexual health.

The Chinese approach

Chinese medical practice incorporates a whole system of techniques and treatments which includes acupuncture, herbs, and breathing exercises. It has proved to be a very powerful and effective form of medicine for a variety of conditions, including problems with the libido.

One of the fundamental tenets of Chinese medical theory is that sexual energy flows around the body, creating spiritual, emotional, and physical well-being. If you can harness this energy, stimulating or regulating its flow, then you hold the key to longevity. For this reason, herbal aphrodisiacs and relaxation techniques have been used for thousands of years in China to promote sexual health.

Energy—"*qi*"—flows through channels known as meridians and can be manipulated by pressure applied at specific points. This practice can also strengthen the energy and clear blockages in the flow caused by physical or emotional problems, as can medicines and certain disciplines such as *qi gung*, t'ai chi, and breathing techniques.

Sexual energy is seen as a manifestation of *jing* (constitutional energy). If your libido is low, it is interpreted as a sign of imbalance or ill health, since depressing the libido is the body's way of conserving *jing*. *Jing* is stored in the kidneys and is called upon during times of tiredness and stress.

You can stimulate certain points, such as BL 23, using a TENS machine (a device used for pain management, especially by women during labor, that sends a mild electric signal) or massage them yourself.

Apply light finger pressure in circular movements, but be careful since some points may feel tender. You can practice this on yourself or your partner and can incorporate a massage as well, if you like. However, as with most of these treatments, it is more sensible to seek the advice of a qualified practitioner, since they can diagnose exactly why you are suffering from a lowered libido and can treat you in a holistic way, taking into account the wider picture.

To my mind, acupuncture—the stimulation of pressure points with needles—is a more effective treatment than acupressure, although it is not something you can self-administer, and you must make sure that your acupuncturist is properly qualified. Someone who has been brought up knowing little about Oriental medicine may be puzzled at first by the fact that acupuncturists concern themselves with parts of the body that seem to have little to do with the problem in hand, but in fact there is a connection. For example, stimulating the spleen meridian can energize the sexual organs, and when ST 36 (four fingers down from the knee, one finger out from the calf bone) is stimulated on both sides at the same time, it alleviates fatigue and increases sexual desire. Stimulation of the ring of fire points (see right) has proved to be very effective, since this increases DHEA levels (see page 21) and therefore strengthens the sex drive.

The ring of fire points

DU 20: on the center of the top of the head
LI 18: on the sides of the neck just below the skull (see left)
SJ 6: two finger widths above the front of the wrist in the middle of the arm
REN 18: in the centre of the chest (on the midline), one finger width above the nipple
BL 23: two finger widths on either side of the spine at the level of the second lumbar vertebra
REN 6: two finger widths directly below the belly button (see below)
REN 1: in the middle of the perineum (between the anus and genitals)
KID 3: in the hollow on the inside of each ankle between the anklebone and the tendon at the back of the ankle

shiatsu

"Shiatsu" is the Japanese word for "finger pressure," although the technique involves massage by the elbow, knee, heel, and fingers at certain points on the body, to treat illness and induce relaxation.

Shiatsu is very similar to acupressure, as it is based on the theory that pressure applied to the meridians can alleviate physical and emotional disturbances by unblocking the flow of energy.

Shiatsu can be used to treat most health problems, including both mild and severe cases of depressed libido and circulatory disorders. It is always best to visit a fully qualified practitioner, but you can practice this simple shiatsu massage described here on yourself or your partner—let them tell you how much pressure to apply.

The sea of intimacy

This exercise stimulates the kidney meridian, which is widely believed to be linked with libido and sexuality.

Place one hand on top of the other just below the navel (the "sea of intimacy" point), and slowly rock your body so that the hands move gently back and forth on your partner's abdomen. Don't rub the skin and check that the pressure you are applying is comfortable. Do this for about three minutes, then gently stop.

homeopathy

Homeopathy perceives medical and emotional problems as signs of inner imbalance, which need to be resolved by treating the underlying cause, rather than individual symptoms. It uses natural remedies to empower the body's own healing capabilities.

These remedies are highly diluted natural substances that would trigger the symptoms in a healthy person if taken at full strength. The reasoning behind this is based on the belief that symptoms are manifestations of the body's attempt to heal itself, so that the more closely a remedy replicates a symptom, the more effectively it heals. Remedies are believed to become more efficacious with every dilution.

Homeopathic remedies are easy to self-prescribe, although it is best to see a qualified practitioner for a thorough diagnosis so that an effective remedy can be selected. One of the most attractive aspects of homeopathic treatment is that it has no side effects and if the wrong remedy is chosen, the worst that will happen is that it won't work (although in some cases remedies will initially aggravate the condition). Nevertheless, if you are taking any other prescribed medicines it is best to seek advice first (never stop

Timeless remedies

Many modern prescription drugs are derived from ancient plant medicines or imitate plant substances. Countless folk remedies have inspired scientific discoveries that help to protect and prolong our health—such as white willow bark, which in 1838 was found to contain salicylic acid, and was synthesized by chemists years later as acetylsalicylic acid (now known as aspirin). The tonics and herbs recommended in this book are taken from many different cultures, whose cures have inspired such research. The World Health Organization now sponsors programs to investigate the medicinal properties of traditional herbal remedies, since it is believed that these may sometimes be more beneficial than Western medicine alone.

taking prescribed medication without informing your doctor). Below is a list of homeopathic medicines that can help increase your libido.

YOHIMBE

This remedy comes from the African yohimbe herb and helps circulate blood in the genitals.

CALCAREA CARBONICA

A remedy made from oyster shells, marble, and chalk or limestone, one of several calcium salts used in homeopathic practice. It is good for premature ejaculation and also helps with loss of libido in women.

ACIDUM PICRINICUM

This remedy is chemically prepared from crystals that are dissolved in alcohol. Try it if you are feeling mentally exhausted, and listless and indifferent toward sex.

CANTHARIS

This preparation is derived from the blister beetle, which secretes the irritant cantharidine if touched. It has long been thought to have aphrodisiac properties, and the Marquis de Sade used to give it to his victims. It is supposed to increase energy during sex.

AGNUS CASTUS

This is a good remedy for erectile dysfunction, premature ejaculation and increasing the libido. Women find it especially useful during the menopause.

SABAL SERRULATA

This remedy comes from the fruit of the saw palmetto, native to North America, and helps with sexual fatigue, boosting the energy circulating in the genitals. It is also prescribed for an enlarged prostate.

LYCOPODIUM CLAVATUM

This plant has been used medicinally since the Middle Ages. It takes its name from the fact that its root looks like a wolf's foot. The remedy helps to get blood moving into a cold, flaccid penis and boost the libido. It can also help with premature ejaculation and prostate problems, and is especially effective if you think symptoms have an emotional or psychological origin.

flower essences

Bottled flower essences are known as "vibrational remedies," said to contain the energy, or imprint, of a particular flower. They work mainly at an emotional level, healing by restoring balance holistically.

Again, you can self-prescribe, although it is usually best to consult a qualified flower essence therapist, as they will make an inclusive diagnosis and recommend treatment for something you might have overlooked or be unaware of.

Many studies have proved the effectiveness of flower essences but none can explain how they work. One

theory is that they stimulate the release of neurotransmitters, which affect all of our bodily processes, including the release of sex hormones, which can boost self-confidence. They are very gentle, subtle, and safe and can be taken with other medication. There are many different types of flower essences, but the ones listed below are particularly relevant to the libido.

Unless otherwise directed, use flower essences by putting seven drops in water and sipping slowly, or placing onto the skin as if it were perfume (on the neck or wrists, for instance). You can also place the drops directly under your tongue—do this twice a day in the morning and evening.

AUSTRALIAN BUSH FLOWER REMEDIES

There are around fifty Australian Bush Flower Remedies at present, discovered by naturopath and kinesiologist Ian White, whose family has specialized in herbal medicine for five generations. Personally, I find these to be very powerful.

BILLY GOAT PLUM Oval, pale green leaves, with fleshy, scented flowers. Much used by the Aborigines, especially for skin problems—problems that can generate feelings of revulsion in others. The flower essence is particularly appropriate for feelings of self-loathing with regard to sex, and for those who have a poor body image. It also helps bring about the realization that sexuality is more than just the physical act and is also spiritual and emotional. It transmutes feelings of shame, ad of the sexual act or genitals being unclean or dirty, into acceptance of the body, sexual pleasure, and enjoyment.

BUSH GARDENIA Round, thick leaves with white, scented flowers. For renewing passion and interest with your partner. It is good for people who are very involved with their own life and tend to take their loved ones for granted. They are brought to face the problem head-on and talk it through with their partner.

CROWEA Dark, pointed leaves with pink, open flowers. This essence takes away the worry that you are not doing things the right way, and strengthens and centers you.

DOG ROSE Small leaves, with flowers that range from deep pink to white. Take this if you feel fearful, since fear blocks and suppresses your sexual vitality, lowers self-esteem, and strengthens resistance to love itself.

BLACK-EYED SUSAN Delicate, rosy blossoms on small shrubs. Helps people be less impatient and more relaxed, still, and present during sex, so that they can fully enjoy the intimacy with their partner.

KANGAROO PAW Green and red flower of a shape resembling the front foot of a kangaroo. This essence will help you to tune in to your partner's needs and to respond with kindness and sensitivity.

WISTERIA A vine with drooping clusters of lilac to purple flowers. Good for women who are finding it difficult to enjoy sex and who feel uncomfortable about their body. It reconnects and opens them up to sensuality, passion, and pleasure; they become willing to trust and share these feelings with their partners. It is also used to help "macho" men rediscover their feminine attributes. Suitable for people who have been the victim of sex abuse.

FLANNEL FLOWER Soft to the touch, with velvety-white flowers tipped with green. To rekindle or enhance the joy of having sex, and allow you to become open to touch and physical and emotional intimacy. It also

Try these Australian Bush Flower combination essences, which use some of the single flower essences mentioned on pages 60–61, to help with sexual problems:

SEXUALITY ESSENCE

Ingredients: BILLY GOAT PLUM, BUSH GARDENIA, FLANNEL FLOWER, FRINGED VIOLET, STURT DESERT ROSE, WISTERIA. This is good for people who feel uptight about sex, or that it is in some way shameful, allowing them instead to feel very comfortable with their body. It also helps to renew passion, sensuality, enjoyment of touch and intimacy, and self-acceptance.

SENSUALITY ESSENCE

Ingredients: BUSH GARDENIA, BILLY GOAT PLUM, FLANNEL FLOWER, LITTLE FLANNEL FLOWER, MACROCARPA, WISTERIA. If you have problems with emotional and physical intimacy, this is one for you, since it encourages you to enjoy passion and sensual fulfillment.

RELATIONSHIP ESSENCE

Ingredients: BLUEBELL, BUSH GARDENIA, DAGGER HAKEA, MINT BUSH, RED SUVA FRANGIPANI, BOAB, FLANNEL FLOWER. This essence releases and clears resentment, blocked emotions and confusion within a rocky relationship. It encourages intimacy and honesty about how you feel. It is good to take this first, followed by sexuality essence.

TIP: If you or anyone you know is suffering from any form of sexual addiction (see page 22), a combination of boab, boronia, bottlebrush, bush iris, flannel flower, and wedding bush is helpful for transforming and resolving the problem.

nurtures gentleness and sensitivity in touching and caressing while helping you to feel comfortable about your body.

LITTLE FLANNEL FLOWER A smaller version of the flannel flower. To help you have fun, to enjoy and experience the playful, spontaneous, and carefree side of sex.

BACH REMEDIES

Edward Bach was a well-known Harley Street (London) physician and bacteriologist who gave up his practice to devote himself to perfecting plant-based remedies. These are not prescribed for the physical complaint, as in conventional medicine, but rather for the patient's state of mind, so that they can participate in their own healing. There are 38 remedies in the Bach pharmacopoeia; below are a few that will help with sexual problems.

ELM This remedy is for those people who are normally quite comfortable with their sexuality, but have begun to feel overwhelmed by the pressure of a relationship and unable to cope.

MIMULUS Mimulus is taken to overcome fear. When fear leads to loss of sex drive, whether this is because of anxiety about inadequacy in bed, about conception, or about pain during intercourse, this may prove an effective treatment.

CRABAPPLE This remedy will rid people of feelings of disgust or uncleanliness. It therefore diminishes the feeling that sex is somehow shameful, and helps you to accept the body—yours and your partner's—for what it is. It may also help to rid us of habits we would rather not have.

OTHER FLOWER ESSENCES

ALPINE LILY Helps women feel comfortable with their body.

HIBISCUS Helps women to get in touch with their feminine sexuality.

STICKY MONKEY FLOWER Helps you to overcome a fear of sexual intimacy that is either repressed or overactive.

Ayurvedic medicine

Ayurvedic medicine is a traditional Indian system that has been around for at least 5,000 years. It is concerned with the attainment of optimum health by living in harmony with nature. One of the ideas upon which it is based is that every single cell of our body contains the same force, or energy (*prana*) that is present in every other living thing, as well as in inanimate objects. Like many other "alternative" medicines, it focuses on re-establishing balance and treats the person holistically. It therefore sees problems with the libido as part of the overall picture. Ayurvedic diagnosis may also attribute low sex drive to increased creative activity. Perhaps your particular difficulty is a psychological response to an unsatisfactory relationship or a sign of poor health. Whatever the diagnosis, an Ayurvedic practitioner will try to balance all the areas of your life using herbal remedies.

aromatherapy

Aromatherapy harnesses the power of highly concentrated plant oils to treat all kinds of conditions. Because the extracts contain the substances that scent the plants, essential oils can be a very sensual way to stimulate the libido.

You can use these oils in the bath, in an oil burner, on a lightbulb, in a bowl of steaming hot water, or in a base oil for a massage. They work quickly, because smell affects the brain almost immediately.

BLACK PEPPER

This aphrodisiac oil adds spice and vitality to your love life. It rekindles the passion when a relationship has cooled through familiarity. Ancient Arabic manuals refer to black pepper's erotic properties, and in Roman times it was used to give men stamina in battle and in the bedroom.

BASIL

A good oil for love, seduction, and fertility. It is an aphrodisiac, awakening the senses and arousing sexual desire. It can be used to revitalize desire in a relationship or if one of you feels anxious or inexperienced. Do not use during pregnancy.

CEDARWOOD

This oil helps to open up the emotions, enabling couples to be very aware during lovemaking, and soothes fears and anxieties surrounding sexuality. Do not use during pregnancy.

CLARY SAGE

This is good for relaxing the muscles, which is why it works as an aphrodisiac. It is calming and can help release inhibitions and relieve fears and anxieties, so this is a good choice if stress is affecting your libido. It is a mild intoxicant that can add a touch of wild abandonment to a night of passion. It used to be used in white magic to entice the interest of a prospective lover. Do not use during pregnancy or heavy periods.

GINGER

Adds vitality to a sexual relationship. It is an aphrodisiac that fires up the libido. It improves circulation, so it is good for erections and the sensitivity of the vagina.

JASMINE

Jasmine has been used by many ancient cultures for rituals, especially sexual ones, and in spells and potions to capture, keep, or rekindle the love of a partner. It can elevate the mood, generate energy and combat frigidity, impotence, and premature ejaculation. It brings strength and warmth to sexual relationships. Do not use during pregnancy.

LAVENDER

In Roman times lavender flowers were strewn over the floor. It was believed their aroma consolidated feelings of desire in relationships and ensured fidelity. Lavender increases blood flow to the genitals, improving erections as well as female sensitivity. It brings calm and peace to a relationship. Do not use during the first three months of pregnancy.

MUSK

In ancient times kings and princes rubbed musk into their hair and beards to give them personal sexual and social power. Today it is added to perfumes and scents to attract the opposite sex.

NEROLI

This is a seductive and sensual oil. Centuries ago it was used by prostitutes in Madrid to seduce their clients. It is a good aphrodisiac and also helps virility.

VETIVER

Calming and stimulating at the same time, this scent is great for sexual adventures.

ORANGE

This gives energy during intimate times, putting the vitality back into love-making. It opens up emotions and brightens relationships, encouraging a mood of joy. Oranges are a symbol of fertility.

TUBEROSE

This flower scent is able to encourage pure lust, and it also helps balance the reproductive systems of both men and women.

ROSE

This is one of my favorite oils. The symbol of love, and favored flower of Aphrodite, goddess of love, the rose is sexually stimulating, as well as healing, and has an uplifting aroma that can help ease the pain of a lost love. It also reveals the tender side of a person's nature. The rose is the flower of seduction—it is traditional to give red roses on Valentine's Day and as a gesture of romantic love. Do not use during pregnancy.

SANDALWOOD

Tantric teachings recommend sandalwood for awakening the sexual energy of the Kundalini (see page 107). It is good as an aphrodisiac and for treating impotence and frigidity. In India it has been used in spiritual and ritualistic sexual practices. If your lovemaking is stuck in a rut, it will help you break out of old sexual patterns and make sex feel new and spontaneous again.

PATCHOULI

Well known for heightening sensual and spiritual awareness, patchouli was popular in the 1960s during the era of free love. It has often been used as an ingredient in love potions and magic charms and is regarded as a potent aphrodisiac.

YARROW FLOWER

This improves blood flow to the penis and vagina, and it helps to strengthen relationships by opening the heart and increasing self-confidence.

YLANG-YLANG

This scent gets people in the mood for sex, since it smells great, relaxes you, and lifts the spirits. It is a powerful aphrodisiac that helps to increase the libido and enhances attraction between lovers—in Indonesia it is traditionally used to scent the nuptial bed to encourage a couple's lust for each other. Ylang-ylang soothes anxiety and raises energy levels and is good for overcoming impotence and frigidity. It opens up the mind to a more sensual and erotic experience during lovemaking.

Sensual aromatherapy baths

Taking a bath can be very therapeutic and soothing, as soaking in warm water cleanses and purifies the skin and eases away stress and tension from the mind and body. It is time spent alone, away from the pressures of the world, family, and work. It is a time of peace and quiet. Pamper yourself by making it special, and add a few ingredients to give your libido a boost later on. You can turn your bathroom into a temple of erotic and luxurious delight. Light candles to help create a relaxing and sensual ambience. Burn some scented oils. Put some freshly cut flowers in a vase. Place crystals around the bath, and add some oils to the water. Slip into the bath and feel the oils soothe and soften your skin.

Powerful combinations of bath oils

Emotional openness: juniper and sandalwood

Aphrodisiac: ylang-ylang and black pepper

Opening the heart: rose and frankincense

Tantalizing: neroli, bergamot, black pepper

Healing sexual tension: in men—clary sage, jasmine, patchouli; in women—jasmine, sandalwood, neroli

Increasing libido: in men—black pepper, ginger, sandalwood; in women—black pepper, ginger, neroli

massage

Touch is essential to our well-being, and massage is basically touch that has a rhythm or pattern. Not only does massage soothe aching muscles, reduce stress, and strengthen the immune system; it also unblocks repressed emotions and increases sexual energy.

Often people forget the importance of sensual touch or massage in a relationship. It can be just gentle teasing or firmer massaging. Tantric teachings often advocate the use of feathers and soft fabrics to tantalize your partner, but this may not be to your taste—perhaps just a plain massage using your hands will prove far more sensual than the sensation of feathers or silk.

Just as the more sex we have, the more we seem to want, so it is the same for touch—the more we have, the more we seem to want and the more we benefit from it. When we touch each other, we release a hormone called oxytocin, which diminishes the level of stress hormones in the body while increasing the sex hormones. It improves a man's erection and the sensitivity of his penis and makes a woman more responsive to sexual attention. If you focus your thoughts on the loving energy emanating from your hands and passing into your partner's body as you give a massage, it can result in an ecstatic as well as a

healing experience for you both. For some people, giving someone a loving massage can be even more intimate than sex.

Couples often use erotic massage as a form of foreplay. You can make it many things—relaxing, exciting, sensual, funny, ticklish, playful—and it can be very helpful if your libido is depressed through stress, tension, boredom, or an inability to relax enough to enjoy sex. Touch can also help a couple to establish a sense of trust; it can be a way for their bodies to attune to one another and achieve a state of relaxation, which is vital during sex. Massage as a form of foreplay, or even just to get in the mood, is also a very good way to reconnect with each other after a busy day apart.

Research suggests that women who don't get enough affectionate physical contact can suffer from depression and a lack of interest in sex, while men become more aggressive and anxious for only sexual touch.

When you massage your lover, you communicate nonverbally. You cannot hide from what your touch communicates, and they cannot hide the response of their skin. Nothing is more relaxing or makes a person feel more open emotionally than a massage from their partner. The very fact that you are spending time and effort on them will make them feel important, pampered, and special.

Try not to make sex the goal of the massage, but instead enjoy the sensation of touch and the intimacy it brings. You may find that sometimes it can make you laugh—or even fall asleep—while at other times it makes you feel very erotic. Just go with the flow, and try not to have an agenda.

To make the massage even more erotic, you can prepare an aromatherapy blend of oils such as jojoba and sweet almond oil with jasmine and bergamot, for men, and neroli and geranium, for women (about 6–10 drops of each). You can also buy many ready-made aphrodisiac blends.

two drops each of rose, black pepper, and ylang ylang) so that the bedroom smells gorgeous.
• A romantic meal is often a good precursor to lovemaking. Let the food look vibrant, and serve it on beautiful plates with elegant cutlery and glasses.

Think of all the things you like and what your partner likes …go to town and truly enjoy yourselves!

Setting the scene

Our surroundings have a powerful impact on the way we feel, and it doesn't take long to create a romantic environment to put you both in the mood for sex. If you do it as a surprise for your partner, you can also refresh a love life that has started to lose its spark.

• Lighting candles is obvious but nevertheless very romantic. The soft light also helps people to feel more comfortable when they undress.
• Scent the room using aromatherapy oils; don't forget to add a few drops of one of the aphrodisiac oils (see page 68).
• You can also make a path of rose petals leading from the front door to the bedroom, with votive lights illuminating the route, or scatter petals on the bed.
• Playing soft romantic music as your partner relaxes after work, during dinner, or during sex itself will help inspire you both.
• Scent your bed sheets with aromatherapy oils (try

Erotic massage

Erotic massage can intensify not only your desire and your response to sexual experiences; it can also add variety to your lovemaking if you feel you are beginning to get stuck in a rut. Although doing things the same old way can feel reassuringly comfortable and familiar, it may prove ultimately destructive, as it can so easily lead to boredom or lack of interest. Erotic massage can also help your inhibitions to dissipate, and encourages experimentation—you may discover new ways to excite your partner that you would not have thought of or bothered with before.

It's important to bear in mind that erotic massage is not a means to an end but, instead, a different way of connecting with and enjoying your partner. It is not a job to get done before you have sex. The longer you spend on your massage, the more intense the pleasure will be for both of you.

Breathing during erotic massage is very important. Try to breathe rhythmically together to create powerful, intimate sensations. The exhalation is as important as the inhalation, as it enables you to surrender at a deeper level.

How to massage

In preparation

- Begin by making sure your partner is comfortable and warm, using sheets, blankets or towels to cover them.
- If you like, you can put a warm towel over the kidney area to help boost sexual energy and also to relax your partner.
- Take off any jewelry that could scratch or hurt your partner.
- Warm your hands.
- Have your massage oil ready.

During the massage

- Run your hands along your partner's body and rest your hands at the top and bottom of the spine—or anywhere on their upper body—just to make the connection with them.
- Massage using the palm of the hand, and repeat each stroke up to 5 times before moving on.
- Don't worry too much about your technique. The important thing is that your partner be comfortable and that the pressure you're applying feels good to them.
- Try to breathe with your partner. Let them lead with their breath, remembering to encourage them to breathe deeply.

To finish

- Rest your hands on your partner's body—at the base of the spine is good—for a few minutes.

Sexual healing massage

Many people are weighed down by powerful and deeply rooted psychological and emotional problems associated with sex. A sexual healing massage is one of the most special gifts a partner can give to their loved one. It will help them to open up and awaken their sexual energy. It is important to remember that erotic massage does not have to involve the genitals; that's entirely up to you. These instructions are only a guide. You can adapt them, use them merely for inspiration, or make up your own massage; so read it through and then improvise. But read it through first—don't hold the book in one hand and massage with the other!

For women

This massage will help to awaken your partner's sexual energy. It will also open her up so that she can experience a more powerful orgasm. Don't be alarmed if she feels upset; this massage can be very intimate, and a very powerful form of sexual healing. Remember to keep checking that she feels okay.

- Make sure she is warm and comfortable. Begin by massaging down both sides of the spine to her lower back. This draws warm energy to the pelvis.
- Gently kiss, rub, or lick the nape of her neck—this is an erogenous zone, and it can be very enjoyable for your partner.
- Ask her to turn over.

- Look into her eyes and harmonize your breathing. Put your left hand on her heart chakra (see page 27) and your right hand on her pelvis (if you're left-handed do this the other way around), and just rest them there for a few minutes.
- Then massage her whole body, brushing energy away from the pelvic area up toward the abdomen and down her arms and legs.
- Move your hands back up to her chest, and massage with your thumbs and/or palms on the center of her chest, using circular movements. This will make her feel calm and open up her heart.
- Move down to her belly and then to the pubic bone, where the base and sacral chakras are found. These are the sexual and creative chakras (see page 27). Massage around her pelvis, her groin, and the tops of her thighs.
- Cup one hand over the pubic area, place the other hand on her heart once more and softly look into her eyes.
- Keeping contact with her body, move your hands down to her feet, and massage her inner legs from the ankles upward.
- Maintain eye contact with her, and when you finish, hold her and cuddle her till she feels relaxed.

For men

Like women, men can have sexual scars as well, and they usually find it harder to talk about them. And there are very few people they can talk to, as it's not generally a topic of conversation with the boys down at the bowling alley! But a loving massage can be a transforming experience and a powerful healing tool. You can massage your partner's scrotum, penis, and perineum, if that is what you both want, but the primary aim of the massage is to heal. It does not matter if the man has an erection or not; he may experience an orgasm, he may not; that is not the point. Bear in mind that it may be difficult for a man to be passive in this situation, but gently try to encourage him to lie back and relax.

- Make sure your partner is warm and comfortable. Massage down both sides of the spine to his lower back. This brings warm energy to the pelvis.
- Gently kiss, rub, or lick the nape of his neck—a powerful erogenous zone for some people.
- Massage his buttocks to help raise his energy levels.
- Ask him to turn over, then place one hand over his heart chakra (see page 27), with the other hand

about 2 inches away from his navel.

- Encourage him to breathe deeply and slowly and match your breathing with his.
- Keeping your breathing synchronized, use both hands to massage the muscles around the pubic bone and groin. Begin above the pubic hair and massage into the groin, then down onto his thighs.
- Encourage your partner to relax and breathe into any sexual energy that may arise.
- Stroke the energy away from the genitals by moving your hands up toward the heart, across his chest, and down his arms to his finger tips and his legs to his feet.
- Retaining contact with his body, move down to his feet. Massage the feet and the inside of the legs.
- Maintaining eye contact, rest your hands on your partner's heart and groin, and let him rest and relax.

The body stroke

This is an ancient Eastern technique, but despite its name there are no complicated strokes to learn. All it requires is for both of you to cover yourselves in massage oil. One of you then lies on top of the other and uses different parts of your body to massage and excite them.

Many people find themselves doing this naturally by using massage oil during their lovemaking and ending up in a sensual, oily embrace. The body stroke is no different and it usually proves to be a very sensuous massage for both partners.

Genital massage

When the genitals are massaged, energy spreads throughout the whole body. Some people follow the techniques religiously, but I don't believe this is necessary—be spontaneous and intuitive, and if you're stuck, see page 142 for suggested reading.

Women are very individual creatures. When it comes to how they like to be touched and massaged, they differ hugely. Let her guide you; ask her to explain or to show you what she enjoys. Make sure she is well lubricated. While massaging her genitals, use your other hand, your mouth, and your tongue to caress and massage other parts of her body.

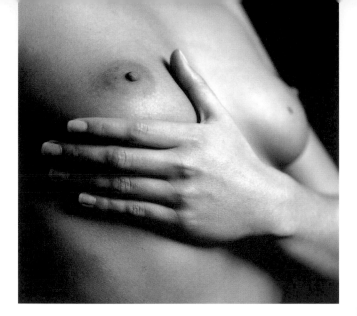

feeling a difference in their body and a heightened sensation in their breasts—even if they have implants! Some women notice a remarked difference in their periods and their libido. Another reason to practice this massage regularly is that it makes you more breast-aware. The density of breast tissue will change throughout the monthly cycle, but if you find a lump that seems at all unusual, you must go and see a doctor.

Breast massage

According to Taoist thought, breast massage moves energy powerfully around a woman's body. This revitalizes the hormonal system and sexual health. Mantak Chia, a Taoist teacher who has written books on the subject, recommends regular self-massage.

- Sit in a comfortable position. Inhale and rub your hands together vigorously, so that you bring energy into your hands and fingers before you start.
- Place your tongue on the roof of your mouth (to create a circuit, which will send energy around your body).
- Use the tips of your second, third, and fourth fingers to massage around the breast (although personally I don't think it is vital that you use only those fingers). The right hand should move clockwise and the left counterclockwise.
- Massage slowly and gently around the breasts, gently pressing on the rib cage.

At first this may seem pointless, and you will probably feel a bit ridiculous, but most women who persist report

If you have never given or received a genital massage before and find the whole concept a little daunting, start by trying a hand or foot massage. Reflexologists believe that the big toe is linked to the pituitary and pineal glands, and according to Tantric thought, stimulation of the pituitary gland harmonizes physical sexual response, and the pineal gland emotional sexual response. Although massaging the fingers or toes may seem a little strange, many people claim that it feels very pleasurable.

CHAPTER THREE

sex tonics

tonic herbs

Most people these days still think of herbs in culinary terms, of use primarily to provide flavor and aroma in cooking. Nevertheless, millions of people around the globe put their trust in herbal medicines, and have done so for many thousands of years. The use of herbal tonics is becoming more widespread every day.

Tonic herbs around the world

CHINA

The Chinese culture is one of the few that has used tonic herbs continuously since ancient times. Archaeological evidence from 2700 B.C. suggests that Peking Man brewed tea and herbs, and they are mentioned in writings dating back to 2000 B.C. Medical documents some 2,000 years old list almost as many herbs, together with observations made by doctors that enabled modern practitioners to use and rely upon the combinations and formulas they

A painting of women collecting and drying herbs in nineteenth-century China.

What makes a tonic herb?

According to both Western and Eastern traditions, a tonic herb
- has been used over many centuries for its healing and life-enhancing properties;
- has no negative side effects when used properly, so that it can be taken regularly to bring about long-term well-being;
- affects the psyche and helps the person spiritually and emotionally;
- tastes good, so that it can become part of a regular diet, if desired.

described. In A.D. 510 T'ao Huang-ching classified 365 herbs that are still used in modern medical practice.

The Chinese are one of many ancient cultures that investigated sexual appetites, since they believe that sexual vitality and healthy bodily function are inextricably linked. Although they advocated boosting the libido through herbal supplements, these were often used for maintaining good health, and were not necessarily aphrodisiacs. An excessively voracious sexual appetite is perceived as an imbalance that could later lead to ill health, just as much as could a weak libido.

The Chinese tonics consist of a unique group of about 50 herbs. They are not curative but are for promoting health. They are also known as "superior herbs." Traditionally, tonics enhanced vitality and longevity. The most unusual ones were used by wealthy people and sages for general wellbeing, to increase their body energy and create "radiant health" —which is achieved in this context in the way we deal with stress. Tonics provide "adaptive" energy that allows us to handle stress more easily, and they regulate bodily, psychic, and spiritual functioning. The Chinese believe that by overcoming stress, we grow as people. Sex tonics improve circulation in the abdominal area and the genitals. They also boost the kidney *yang* energy, responsible for strengthening the libido.

AFRICA AND THE MIDDLE EAST

There are many references to herbal medicines in ancient Egyptian and Babylonian writings. Cloves were found in Tutankhamun's tomb, and garlic was fed to the men who built the pyramids. Arab healers used herbal distillations over 1,000 years ago, and inherited and refined the Greek medical systems. The medicines of precolonial Africa were plant based, and secret societies today ingest similar intoxicating plants in religious rituals.

A woodblock engraving of an ancient Egyptian herb garden.

chapter three: sex tonics

The therapeutic properties of some of the African herbs are now supported by modern scientific research. Yohimbe (see page 84) has aphrodisiac and stimulatory properties, and pygeum bark is good for treating disorders of the prostate.

INDIA

Plant medicine is mentioned in the *Vedas*—an ancient Hindu text dating from 1000 B.C. Ayurveda is the ancient Indian herbal medical system that is said to have originated with the Hindu gods. In 1100 the *Characka samia* recorded about 500 herbal preparations that are still used today. The Indian *De Materia Medica* lists about 2,000 herbs.

THE WEST

The ancient civilisations of Greece and Rome both used herbal medicines. Hippocrates (c. 460–377/359 B.C.) made clinical observations of disease and responses to herbs. Galen (Claudius Galenus, c. 130–201 A.D.), physician to the Roman emperors, wrote extensively on medical matters, including a treatise on herbs and their individual therapeutic uses. The *De Materia Medica*, written in the first century but used in Europe up until the seventeenth century, was written by a Greek physician and lists 950 medicines—of which 650 were herbal. There are texts from Anglo-Saxon times that describe many medicinal herbs, but after the Renaissance many herbal medicines were dismissed as the province of witches and wise women. These women were healers, bonesetters and midwives, who kept notebooks of recipes and observations—and many were persecuted for practicing their art.

European settlers arriving in the Americas brought with them their knowledge of herbal medicines, into which the plant lore of the Native Americans became absorbed over time. Sound guidance regarding the dosage and the safety of hundreds of herbs was included in the twentieth-century edition of the U.S. pharmacopoeia, *National Formulary*, although most were omitted from the 1950s onward. These days the United States is one of the countries that lead the world in the promotion of tonic and therapeutic herbs.

LATIN AMERICA

The traditional herbal medicines of Latin America have roots in the indigenous cultures. South American medical documents discovered by Spanish and Portuguese explorers included lists of herbal medicines. Western scientists are trying to preserve the wisdom of the traditional Amazon healers by sponsoring shamans. Some of the herbs presently under scrutiny are cat's claw (extracted from plants belonging to the Peruvian *Rubiaceae* family), *pau d'arco* (so named by the Portuguese, who first colonized Brazil) and guarana.

A word of caution…

If you are suffering from any illness, seek medical advice from a doctor or herbal practitioner before taking any herbal tonic. If you take a tonic and think that you are suffering from a reaction to it, stop at once and seek the advice of a qualified practitioner.

Herbal tonics for the libido

All the herbs in this section have a long history of many and varied uses, but I have concentrated here only on their effects on sex and the libido. They can be used by themselves or as a preparation with other herbs made by a qualified herbalist.

Please note that herbs do not turn men into super-studs, or women into voracious love goddesses, but they are recognized for treating sexual dysfunction and low libido. Herbal aphrodisiacs can heighten sensation in the genitals, stimulate hormones and glandular secretions, and promote circulation. This should result in a noticeable increase in energy, vitality, and sexual potency.

As with any herbal therapy, for the best results aphrodisiacs should be taken over a period of time; they work with the body's circulatory and hormonal systems, which take a while to change. You may have to wait two to three months before you notice an improvement.

Tonic herbs are safe for long-term use as a nutritional supplement since they are nontoxic, are harmless to all organs, and protect against disease. They are very nutritious for both the blood and the organs, and help maintain balance within the body, which is so vital for good health.

AGNUS CASTUS

Agnus castus berries correct hormone imbalances and thus restore sexual energy levels, healthy desire, and performance. Don't overdo it, however, since it can also have the opposite effect—one of its other names is chasteberry, and, according to legend, monks used to chew its leaves to help them keep their vows of celibacy. Do not take if you are pregnant or breast-feeding.

ASHWAGANDA

An Ayurvedic Indian herb that can be used as a sex tonic for men. Unlike ginseng, ashwaganda does not raise blood pressure.

DAMIANA LEAF

Damiana leaf has been used for thousands of years as an aphrodisiac, a remedy for impotence, and a nerve tonic (its Latin name is *Tunera aphrodisiaca*). It is believed to contain alkaloids that raise testosterone levels and act as a stimulant tonic for both the male and female reproductive systems. It is good for sexual problems relating to stress and inhibition, since it can produce a mild euphoria (so do not drive until you know how it affects you). It has a pleasant taste and smell. Do not take if you are pregnant or breast-feeding. Excessive amounts may harm the liver.

HORNY GOAT WEED

It is said that this herb acquired its name after a curious goatherd realized that mating among the herd increased after his goats had been eating it. It is now known to be a powerful male aphrodisiac, improving circulation and stimulating hormone production. Recent studies indicate that sperm count and semen density increase in just a few hours after taking it. It is said to be one of the strongest herbs for sexual potency in the entire ancient Chinese

Velvet elk antler

Velvet elk antler has been used in China as a supplement for thousands of years and is deemed as important as ginseng. It boosts energy, prevents premature aging, and strengthens the immune system. The antlers are taken each year from specially bred elks during the rapid growth phase of antler development. It helps improve sex drive by increasing testosterone, raises energy levels, and acts as an antidepressant. People also take it for impotence and PMS. It is advisable to see a herbalist before self-prescribing velvet elk antler.

pharmacopoeia, where it is known as a warm herb that generates *jing* energy in the kidneys. Horny goat weed is also thought to be helpful for women whose lack of sex drive can be attributed to fatigue, stress, illness or hormone imbalance.

GOTU KOLA

Gotu kola grows in Madagascar, India, Sri Lanka and South Africa, and is available in capsule, cream, or tincture form. It strengthens the veins and capillaries and therefore improves the flow of blood to the genitals, increases sex drive, and lifts depression. Do not use it if you are pregnant or breast-feeding, or have a history of skin inflammation.

GINGKO BILOBA

This herb has excited much interest recently, since tests seem to indicate that it improves the memory and brain function, but it has been a staple of Chinese medicine for thousands of years. *Gingko biloba* improves circulation and blood flow to the pelvic area and therefore strengthens erectile function. It can also help with impotence brought on by anti depressants.

GINSENG

Ginseng is one of the most popular tonic herbs; people take it primarily to increase their energy and stamina. However, it has been used for thousands of years as a safe and effective sex tonic. Its compounds work on the pituitary-adrenal axis to boost sexual potency, reduce the effects of stress and balance the hormones. There are many different types of ginseng. Red panax (Korean) ginseng is the strongest aphrodisiac but can raise blood pressure in some people if they take too much. If you have high blood pressure, consult a herbalist before you take ginseng. Do not use it if you are pregnant or breast-feeding.

GOKHRU FRUIT

Gokhru fruit is used to restore sexual potency and desire by boosting levels of testosterone. Traditionally it has been used as a herb to treat impotence and premature ejaculation, as well as other genitally related problems, such as urinary tract infections.

MACA

Maca is a Peruvian herb that helps erectile function by normalizing steroid hormone levels, and increases sex drive in both sexes. Peruvians have used maca as a sex-enhancing herb for centuries, and they also believe it is good for increasing energy, vaginal lubrication and mental clarity, and reducing the mood swings of PMS. It improves fertility, immunity, and stamina, while also balancing hormones.

MUIRA PAUAMA

Originating in the Amazonian rain forests, this herb has traditionally been used as an aphrodisiac and tonic for rheumatism and muscle paralysis. It is also believed to maintain testosterone levels.

The Chinese believe tonic herbs promote a slower aging process and longevity; radiant health; strength; happiness; wisdom; physical vitality; mental acuity; adaptability; sex drive; love; compassion; and harmonious relationships.

NETTLE ROOT

Recent research suggests that nettle root can benefit sex drive by freeing testosterone from its carrier protein. Exsativa, a herbal formula made of *Avena sativa* (spring oats), stinging nettle, and sea buckthorn, can help increase sexual desire, performance, and activity. Nettles contain iron, so are good for people who are low in energy and thus apathetic about sex.

effects, however, so consult a qualified herbalist before you take yohimbe. Do not take if you suffer from cardiovascular disease or psychological problems.

SAW PALMETTO BERRY

These berries are produced by the dwarf American palm, found in the sand dunes of the Atlantic and Caribbean coasts, and can be eaten or taken as tablets, capsules, teas, or liquid extract. They are a sexual stimulant supposed to work directly on the sex hormones. Saw palmetto berry is known best for its ability to shrink an enlarged prostate, which can interfere with normal sexual function. It is also an effective treatment for impotence, prostatitis, and male fertility problems. It increases blood flow to the genitals and promotes sexual health in general.

SARSAPARILLA ROOT

Since the 1600s, sarsaparilla has enjoyed a worldwide reputation as an aphrodisiac and male tonic. It was particularly well known to the Indians of Mexico and South America, who used it as a tonic for general weakness and to improve sexual performance. It enhances the libido by stimulating the production of testosterone and progesterone.

YOHIMBE BARK

Yohimbe is a West African tree native to Cameroon, Congo, and Gabon, and is used as a potent aphrodisiac. It dilates the blood vessels of the skin, counteracting low blood pressure and improving blood flow to the genitals. This herb specifically increases male energy and libido, making erections easier to achieve. There is a host of possible side

tonic recipes

The recipes that follow use drops of liquid extracts (unless otherwise stated), as herbs in this form blend together more easily and tend to taste better. All the ingredients you require are available from herbalists or good health shops (see page 140 for some useful addresses).

ADVENTURES OF ADAM

This is a great *yang* tonic for male sexual vigour and appetite. When you are ready to drink, you can place a cinnamon stick in the glass and stir to add a little extra warmth and spice.

Serves 1
1 cup apple juice
20 drops red ginseng
20 drops *Avena sativa* (spring oats)
1 cinnamon stick (optional)

In a small saucepan, mix together the liquids and heat gently over a low flame. Pour into a tall glass and stir. Serve the drink warm or allow it to cool. Garnish with the cinnamon stick, if you like.

What if I don't want to make my own sex tonic?

You can buy ready-made tonics from a number of health centers and herbalists (see page 140), which you mix yourself at home with soda water, or take daily as a tincture, depending on what you prefer. You might be surprised at how good they taste!

½fl oz Wu Wei Zi
½fl oz Gan Cao

For two people, mix 1–2 tablespoons of the tonic with any fruit juice(s) and serve with ice.

EVE OF ROMANCE

This is a tonic to help women get in the mood for sex.

Serves 1

¼ cup papaya juice
¼ cup pineapple juice
¼ cup orange juice
20 drops kava kava
20 drops damiana
20 drops red ginseng
1 wedge of orange
1 wedge of pineapple

Put all the liquid ingredients in a blender, and blitz to a smooth consistency. Serve over ice, and garnish with the orange and pineapple wedges.

AFTERGLOW

This is an after-sex tonic for both men and women. Based on Taoist concoctions, which promote longevity, it opens the heart chakra and enhances the feelings that people experience following sex. Don't worry if the names of the herbs look a little daunting—you can take this list into any Chinese herbalist or health shop and they will happily make up a bottle for you.

Makes ½ pint

¼ cup Xi Yang Shen
¼ cup Tai Zi Shen
⅕ cup Sang Shen
⅛ cup Bai Zi Ren
⅛ cup Gou Qi Zi
½ fl. oz. Ling Zi
½ fl. oz. Lian Zi
½ fl. oz. Huang Jing

CHAPTER FOUR

aphrodisiac foods

a healthy diet

Many foods are reputed to have aphrodisiac qualities, and it just so happens that a good proportion of these have been found to be high in nutrients as well; to maintain a healthy sex drive, you need a diet rich in vitamins, minerals, and essential fatty acids.

This is especially true if your libido is low because of stress, tiredness, ill health, smoking, or excessive alcohol intake. Unfortunately, most of the food we eat today, especially in the West, is highly processed, and lacks much of the necessary goodness, so choose fresh ingredients rather than processed foods and try to buy organic when you can. Include lots of fruit, vegetables, and whole grains in your diet and don't skip meals.

The food of love

Be it because of their nutritional benefits, or because of their shape, color, associations, moisture content, or the way the taste lingers in the mouth, the following foods are definitely considered to be aphrodisiacs. The important thing to remember when you are using food to spice things up in the bedroom is to have fun. Feed each other hot buttered asparagus spears or rich Belgian chocolates. Experiment and let yourself go.

ANISEED/STAR ANISE

In ancient India a paste of powdered aniseed and star anise was combined with honey and spread on the genitals to make an explosive aphrodisiac paste. Ancient Romans also used to add aniseed to wedding cakes to send the newlyweds off on a high! Modern research has indicated that it may help to combat fatigue.

APPLES

Ever since biblical times, apples have been seen as a symbol of temptation. In the West they are also perceived as a symbol of love, as they were the favorite fruit of Rhiannon, the Celtic goddess of love.

ARTICHOKES

The French advocate the eating of artichoke because it is good for relationships. Perhaps this is because of its flower-like shape, and the way that it is eaten; the leaves are stripped one by one until its heart is revealed.

ASPARAGUS

Asparagus has been regarded as an aphrodisiac since the days of the ancient Egyptians, Greeks, and Romans, perhaps because of its phallic shape. In the seventeenth-century English physician Nicholas Culpeper (whose books formed the basis of herbalism in the English-speaking world) decreed that "a decoction of asparagus roots could stirreth up bodily lust in man and woman."

chapter four: aphrodisiac foods

and pine nuts (as in pesto sauce), although there has been no recent research to support this. Basil does, however, significantly reduce blood sugar and therefore improve overall health.

BELGIAN ENDIVE

In medieval times Belgian endive was added to love potions, as people believed it promoted fidelity.

BLACK PEPPER

Black pepper is the most common spice, and has been used for thousands of years in medicinal preparations in countries from ancient Greece to India. It contains chromium (see page 51) and has been prescribed for a host of ailments, although can be generally recommended for overall well-being.

BANANAS

Definitely an aphrodisiac, and not just because of the shape! Bananas increase the libido because they contain an alkaloid (bufotenine) that lifts the spirits and helps with self-confidence. Bufotenine is found mainly just under the skin, so a good dish to make is bananas baked in their skin. Because bananas are naturally high in carbohydrate, they give you energy. They are also rich in potassium.

BASIL

Mexicans and Italians think of basil as a strong aphrodisiac, especially when it is combined with garlic

CARROTS

The ancient Greeks called carrots *philon*, which means "loving." They gave carrots to people they wanted as their sexual partner, in the hope that it would make the desire reciprocal…. It may sound strange to us now, but orgies involved a lot of carrot eating as it was believed that the whole plant served as an aphrodisiac.

CAVIAR

Everyone knows that caviar is thought to be an aphrodisiac, but not many people know why. Some believe it is the strong smell and flavor, which are supposed to remind men of women's genitals….

Personally I think that's nonsense; I opt for the explanation that it might contain steroid compounds, which, in very large quantities, help boost sex drive. Or maybe it's just the idea of self-indulgence and decadence that lies behind its association with sex.

CELERY

Celery tonics and elixirs have been made for many thousands of years—in ancient Greece they were offered as an award at athletic games. Celery is thought to be an aphrodisiac because it contains a substance similar to a pig's pheromone, which also boosts the sex drive of humans. It is a diuretic, however, so watch your fluid intake.

CHOCOLATE

In the court of King Louis XV of France, chocolate was eaten regularly as a sexual stimulant. It increases

mood-enhancing chemicals in your brain, especially PEA (see page 23). PEA gives you a slight confidence buzz—that is until the weight piles on from too much chocolate! Chocolate is addictive because of the chemicals it releases into your system. It contains tryptophan, which converts to serotonin (see page 25) and makes you feel happy. It also contains theobromine, which lifts your spirits. You may be glad to learn that it is also nutritious, since it is high in magnesium and potassium. It makes you feel "blissed out" since it contains PEA, which is often dubbed the love chemical. This can be detected in the system of people who are in love or who have just experienced an orgasm. It also stimulates the production of endorphins, which act as very mild opiates. Dark chocolate is better than milk, since it contains more cocoa and is therefore richer in minerals, antioxidants, and feel-good chemicals. All of this, together with its smell, taste, and texture and the way it melts seductively on your fingers and in your mouth, makes eating it an all-around sexual experience …or so the advertisements for chocolate would have us believe. Now there are plenty of excuses to indulge in your favorite treat; and if you

Offering a sensual feast

When food is lovingly prepared and beautifully presented, it is a delight to all the senses.

- Prepare bite-size foods that can be eaten with the fingers.
- Avoid fatty foods and heavy carbohydrates, since these cause drowsiness.
- Decorate the table with flowers and candles.
- As for the food itself, think about asparagus, smoked salmon, strawberries, peeled grapes, fresh mango slices, dark chocolate, olives, oysters …lots of flavors, aromas, colors, and textures.
- Sauces are seen as sensual as they drip off the food over your partner's lips and onto the plate. Bear in mind, however, that for some people this can be a major turn-off!

tell your partner it increases your sex drive, you'll be given chocolates every night!

DURIANS

Most people have probably never seen a durian. It's an oval fruit with a hard, spiny rind, which despite a slightly odd smell has a pleasant taste. It is so popular in Thailand, the Philippines, Malaysia, and Borneo that it is rarely exported, so you may have quite a job getting hold of one. In its native countries it is well known for its aphrodisiac qualities. In Malaysia they say: "When Durians fall, the sarongs rise."

EGGPLANTS

It is in India that eggplants are thought to be an aphrodisiac. The *Kama Sutra* recommends that you rub eggplant juice on your lover's body for a month…but think twice about this, because it may not do much for you!

EGGS

Eggs—especially fertilized free-range eggs—contain steroid substances that enhance the libido. Throughout history people have believed that eating eggs would help them sexually.

FENNEL

In the 1930s scientists contemplated using fennel as a source of estrogen, since it contains estragole—an estrogen-like substance. This has been seen to

GARLIC

Garlic is well known for strengthening your immune system, helping to lift your spirits, and boosting your sex drive. It improves sexual stamina by increasing circulation to all parts of the body. Be careful, however, as its smell is known to ward off partners as well as vampires! Garlic is listed in the Chinese pharmacopoeia as a potent aphrodisiac. It contains the stimulant allin.

increase sex drive. Fennel is also supposed to help with childbirth and menstruation, enhance erections, and prolong male orgasm. It is said that fennel stimulates the genitals of whoever eats it, as well as increasing desire. Since it is widely held that the way to a man's heart is via his stomach, perhaps fennel should be on the menu when you first cook for him!

FENUGREEK

Fenugreek grows in countries along the eastern shore of the Mediterranean. Herbalists prescribe the seeds for a variety of disorders, since they are thought to be a good tonic. Besides acting as an aphrodisiac, they are very cleansing.

FIGS

Figs are certainly associated with fertility because in some cultures they are thrown at newlyweds instead of rice or confetti. Some people thinks figs are erotic because of their appearance. I'm not so sure myself!

GINGER

Ginger root is warming and stimulating. It improves circulation and spices up your sex life. It is one of the best-known aphrodisiacs.

HONEY

In ancient India people used to make a poultice with honey and smear it on the penis, believing that it would increase its size! Women would also mix honey

chapter four: aphrodisiac foods

LOBSTER

Lobster and crayfish are thought to be good aphrodisiacs. Some believe this is just because they are an expensive delicacy, but seafood is also a good source of zinc (see page 47), which is vital for a healthy libido.

MANGO

There is a belief, originating in India, that mango increases the libido and can make sex last longer.

MELON

In Persia melon was thought to increase your appetite for love—and food—if eaten regularly enough, making sense of the convention of offering melon as an appetizer to a meal.

with crocodile feces, olive oil, and lemon juice to use as a contraceptive pessary. That sounds bad enough to prevent sex altogether! It's much better ingested— apart from the fact that it tastes delicious, it contains bee pollen (see page 49).

LEEKS

Leeks have been thought of as an aphrodisiac for years, maybe because of their family relationship with onions and garlic.

LICORICE

According to folklore, licorice root enhances the libido. This could be because it contains compounds that are needed to produce female hormones, such as a corticosteroid (a hormone that helps produce estrogen).

MUSHROOMS

In ancient Greece and Rome, raw mushrooms were considered an aphrodisiac, as their smell was thought to be reminiscent of sex. Mushrooms are a good source of B vitamins (see page 48).

NUTMEG

Besides counteracting a low libido, nutmeg can help with nervous disorders and depression. A concoction of grated nutmeg mixed with avocado, left to chill overnight, is supposed to stimulate sexual arousal.

OATS

Oats are an aphrodisiac that can be taken in supplement form if you don't wish to eat them. They are also used to treat certain addictions, such as smoking, which are damaging to the libido.

The dictionary defines an aphrodisiac as "something that arouses sexual desire." How can food excite sexual desire? It needs to look sensual or sexual, smell sumptuous, and taste orgasmic! The *Encyclopedia Britannica* states: "The visual satisfaction . . .of appetizing food . . .the olfactory stimulation . . .and the tactile gratification tend to bring on a state of euphoria conducive to sexual expression."

OYSTERS

Oysters are one of the best-known aphrodisiac foods, most probably because of their high zinc content (which is important for increasing the libido and for male sexual potency), salty taste, and marine smell. Some people think they also look like the female genitals. For pure decadence, they are best enjoyed with champagne. The Chinese believe they should be eaten fresh and raw for optimum effect as raw oysters contain a number of active enzymes and hormones.

PEACHES

The peach has been used as a cure for a whole range of ailments. The ancient Chinese believed the peach to be an aphrodisiac, and its sensual shape and soft skin have helped maintain its reputation.

PASSION FRUIT

Perhaps the name is enough to do the trick.

PEANUTS

Peanuts are thought to trigger the orgasm response and make orgasms stronger because of their histidine content.

ONIONS

Ancient Egyptian priests, who had taken a vow of celibacy, were forbidden onions, as they were thought to be such a powerful aphrodisiac. In France, onion soup was given to restore energy and rekindle the spark after the wedding night.

PINE KERNELS

Pine nuts were thought to be an aphrodisiac as far back as ancient Roman times, and recent research would seem to substantiate their theory.

POMEGRANATES

The pomegranate is also known as the love apple. It has high levels of vitamin C and potassium, which promote circulation, and has been used as an aphrodisiac since ancient times. It also contains a form of oestrogen called estrone, which boosts the libido. The *Kama Sutra* recommends that couples split open a pomegranate and share it to enjoy an unforgettable night of passion and increased fertility.

PRUNES

In the old days brothels used to serve prunes to prostitutes and clients in order to keep up their sex drive. Be careful, however, since large quantities can cause an upset stomach.

SAFFRON

The Spanish, Indians, and Chinese believe that saffron helps men with their sexual performance.

SAUERKRAUT

Reputedly an aphrodisiac for men, sauerkraut—finely shredded and pickled cabbage—helps to increase sex drive and performance because of its high content of vitamin C and lactic acid.

SESAME SEEDS

Because of their high EFA content (see page 47), sesame seeds are used in China to help with fertility.

There is also an aphrodisiac preparation used in Arabic countries that combines sesame seeds with ginger, cloves, nutmeg, coriander, cardamom, and lavender.

SHRIMP

As with other shellfish, shrimp are a notable aphrodisiac because of their high zinc content, which is essential for sexual appetite and fertility. Indeed, a dish of shrimp and sesame seeds is traditionally served at Cantonese wedding ceremonies.

STRAWBERRIES

Strawberries and champagne are thought to be a great aphrodisiac combination. Strawberries are known as the fruit of Venus, the Roman goddess of love.

TRUFFLES

Truffles are often sniffed out by sows on heat because they smell like the pheromones of the male pig. Both white and black truffles are said to be equally strong…and delicious! They are soft, exotic—and expensive—and can make a meal seem just a little more special.

VANILLA

Vanilla is said to be a strong aphrodisiac, and is often used in perfumes as well as in cooking.

aphrodisiac recipes

MANGO, WHITE PEACH, AND MELON SALAD WITH TOASTED OATS, PUMPKIN SEEDS, AND HONEYED GREEK YOGURT

Fresh fruit is full of vitamin C, while many seeds contain essential fatty acids and zinc. If you have trouble finding white peaches, simply substitute with any other peach variety. From India you can order, via the internet, a wonderful variety of mango called "Alphonso." It is a fabulous-tasting fruit, and its juices would work beautifully in this dish.

Serves 2
1 cup rolled oats
¼ cup pumpkin seeds
1 tablespoon light brown granulated sugar
1 tablespoon maple syrup
1 ripe mango, peeled
2 ripe white peaches, halved and stoned
1 ripe melon, peeled, halved and deseeded
1¾ cups Greek yogurt
4 tablespoons clear honey

For the toasted oats and seeds, preheat the oven to 325°F. Mix the oats with the seeds, sugar, and maple syrup, then transfer to a baking tray and bake in the oven for 15–20 minutes. Remove from the oven, stir well, and bake for another 10–15 minutes until crisp and golden. Leave to cool.

Cut the mango flesh and the peach halves into thin strips and place in a large bowl. Then cut the melon into thin wedges and add to the bowl. Put the yogurt in another bowl and stir in the honey.

Mix the fruit well and sprinkle with the cooled toasted oats and seeds. Divide between two bowls and serve with a few dollops of the honeyed yogurt.

AVOCADO, FENNEL, AND CARROT SALAD WITH CRÈME FRAÎCHE VINAIGRETTE

Serves 2
2 ripe avocados, halved and stoned
1 large head of fennel, trimmed and thinly sliced
2 carrots, grated
For the vinaigrette:
2 tablespoons white wine vinegar
4 tablespoons olive oil
Juice of ½ lemon
2 teaspoons crème fraîche
Salt and freshly ground black pepper
Few sprigs of parsley, chopped
1 teaspoon chopped chives

Start by making the vinaigrette. Combine all the ingredients in an empty, lidded jar. Screw the lid on, shake well, and set aside while you prepare the salad.

Carefully peel the avocado halves and slice each half into eighths lengthwise. To serve, arrange the avocado, fennel slices, and grated carrot on two plates. Shake the vinaigrette again, and drizzle over the salad.

GRILLED SOLE WITH ROAST ASPARAGUS, BABY LEEKS, AND HOLLANDAISE SAUCE

This dish is great for the libido, since ocean fish has high levels of essential fatty acids and zinc. Asparagus and creamy hollandaise are a perfect combination. (Because hollandaise is a butter-based sauce, there is always a risk of curdling. Should this happen, a tablespoon of boiling water will do wonders in bringing it back. This also works if the sauce separates when left to keep warm.)

Serves 2

10 asparagus spears
10 baby leeks, trimmed
Olive oil, for roasting
2 sole, or flounder, weighing about 1lb each
1 tablespoon unsalted butter, melted

For the hollandaise sauce

2 egg yolks
$1/8$ cup white wine
$1\,3/4$ sticks unsalted butter, melted
Juice of 1 lemon
Salt and freshly ground pepper

Preheat the oven to 350°F.

Begin by making the sauce. Bring some water in a pan to simmering point. Put the yolks and wine in a stainless-steel bowl over the hot water and whisk until the mixture doubles in size and thickens. But be careful not to leave the bowl suspended over the hot water for too long.

Remove from the heat and gradually whisk in the melted butter. The sauce will start to thicken even more. When the butter has mixed in, add the lemon juice and seasoning and keep warm while you prepare the remainder of the dish.

Lay the asparagus and leeks in a roasting tray, drizzle with a little olive oil and season well. Place in the oven for 15 minutes or until tender. They may take less time depending on their thickness.

Meanwhile, preheat the broiler. Trim the fins and tails off the fish and brush with the melted butter. Season, place on a buttered baking tray, and cook under the broiler for 6–7 minutes or until the skin starts to crisp and the butter turns golden.

Arrange the asparagus and leeks on two plates, carefully place the sole on top, and pour the lemony hollandaise over. Serve immediately.

STIR-FRIED GARLIC AND GINGER SHRIMP WITH SESAME SEEDS, SHITAKE MUSHROOMS, AND GREEN ONIONS

Serves 2

16 large raw shrimp, peeled and deveined, tails left on
2-inch piece fresh gingerroot, peeled and finely grated
2 garlic cloves, peeled and finely chopped
1 tablespoon Chinese rice wine or dry sherry
1 tablespoon dark soy sauce
1/4 teaspoon sesame oil
2 tablespoons peanut oil
1/4 teaspoon light brown granulated sugar
1/4 cup chicken stock
7 oz. shitake mushrooms, roughly chopped
2 tablespoons sesame seeds
3 green onions, sliced on the diagonal

With a sharp knife, cut along the back of each shrimp from the head to the tail and open out into a butterfly shape. Place in a bowl along with the ginger, garlic, rice wine or sherry, soy sauce, and sesame oil. Cover and leave to marinate in the refrigerator for 1 hour.

Heat the peanut oil in a large wok, and add the shrimp together with the marinade. Stir-fry for 2 minutes or so and add the sugar.

Pour in the chicken stock and simmer until the shrimp are just tender. Finally, add the mushrooms and sesame seeds, and stir-fry for another minute or so. Stir well to combine, and serve immediately, sprinkled generously with the green onions.

CHAPTER FIVE

healing
positions

do we need healing?

Sex is everywhere these days. We are bombarded with sexual imagery in the media. It is used all the time in advertising, is readily available on the internet and television, and is splashed all over the covers of magazines. So why, in this age of sexual liberation, are so many of us not enjoying it?

The problem is that we are under immense pressure to perform—to make sure we're doing it right, having enough of it, and relishing every minute of it. And who can blame us for trying too hard when we seemingly have so much to live up to? People become addicted to the sex they see in photographs and on screen, fantasizing to such an extent that this unreal view of sex takes control over real life.

Tantra is one of the ways people can begin to relax and enjoy sex again on an intimate level. It can help you to unwind, and feel more confident and respectful of yourself and your partner, while helping you to rekindle passion and desire.

"Some people say tantric sex is sex education for grown-ups. And we certainly need it."

Val Sampson, author

But what is Tantra?

Tantra originated among the ancient tribes of India around 5,000 years ago, and was first documented in the sixth century. The name comes from a Sanskrit word meaning "weaving" and also "expansion." The simple explanation of Tantra is that it gives women self-esteem and sexual confidence and men the ability to become multi-orgasmic, but there is a little more to it than that. Tantra became popular in the West in the 1960s in a modified version known as "Neo-Tantra," which couples exercises with psychotherapy techniques to increase sex drive and intimacy in relationships.

Many people associate the word "Tantra" with weird positions and endlessly long sex. In fact, Tantra is about the flow and exchange of powerful sexual energy within the body. Taoist thought (see page 115) claims that the embracing of the libido is a path to enlightenment, and sex is seen as a route to spiritual transformation and growth. Tantra practitioners try to awaken Kundalini energy—the dormant spiritual power visualized as a coiled snake lying at the base of the spine—and direct it upward to unite with Shiva energy (pure consciousness manifesting in creative union) at the crown of the head. Sex can thus reintegrate the body and mind, transforming physical passion into spiritual ecstasy.

One of the most attractive aspects of Tantric sex is that couples worship each other as embodiments of divine male and female principles, leaving the gender

Your experience of Kundalini energy can be enhanced not just through Tantric sex but also through the practice of yoga and meditation (see pages 43 and 45), during which you can visualize moving energy around the body.

choose. It shows partners how to satisfy each other in the most intense, intimate, and meaningful ways. It enables new lovers to get to know each other on a deeper level, while couples who have been together for years can rekindle the spark and rediscover the passion and intimacy they may have lost.

Tantra shows you that sex need not just be a physical event, a fumble in the dark in which orgasm is the only goal; but instead, it allows you to experience intimacy, love, respect and trust on a whole new level. You just have to be prepared to open your mind to what it can do… .

politics and power struggles that so beleaguer Western society far behind. Even the language used in tantric texts is more respectful than it is in the West. It says something about Western culture that the names for the genital organs are among the most powerful forms of verbal abuse! In tantric writings, however, "*yoni*"—the word for the vagina—means "sacred palace" and is seen as the source of universal bliss. "*Vajra*," the word for the penis, means "tool of consciousness." If only all men used it as such!

So how can tantra help me?

If sexual desire has diminished or evaporated completely in your relationship, for whatever reason, tantra teaches you that excitement lives in each of us all the time and can be accessed whenever we

Tantric tasters

If you're not sure whether you would like to pursue Tantra any further, why not try the following easy exercises?

- The next time you are approaching orgasm, breathe deeply. Don't do what most people do, which is to hold their breath, tighten or clench their muscles, and will the orgasm to happen! Your orgasm will be more intense if you can relax and breathe deeply.
- The next time you are having sex or experiencing orgasm, try to visualize the energy moving around your body, away from your genitals. Just relax and imagine it moving up your spine. If you can, keep your tongue touching the roof of your mouth, as this helps the energy to circulate.

Tantric exercises

If you are interested in learning more about Tantra, here are some gentle exercises to begin with. Familiarize yourselves with them beforehand so you won't find that you have to refer to the book every five seconds!

Eye gazing

Eye gazing is one of the best ways for a couple to tune in to each other and forge an intimate connection.

Sit opposite each other, and gaze softly and lovingly into each other's eyes. Look more deeply, as if you are trying to see into each other's soul. Breathe together to increase the feeling of connection.

How do I concentrate?

Some people say that it doesn't feel natural to have to concentrate on what they are doing to be able to enjoy sex to the full. Cast your mind back, however, to when you were younger and having your first sexual experiences. Sex probably didn't feel at all natural until you were more familiar with what you were doing and had found your own rhythm. It's the same when you're learning Tantric sex. At first it feels strange, but then it just comes naturally. So don't worry if you spend your first few attempts at Tantra in fits of laughter—it just adds to the fun.

Creating energy circuits

Sit opposite each other with your knees touching. Place your right palms on each other's heart chakra (see page 27), and place your left hand over each other's right hand. Look into each other's eyes and breathe together. Put your foreheads together, close your eyes, and enjoy the intimacy between you.

   Concentrate on the loving energy flowing out of your hearts and back in through your hands, creating an energy circuit. Try complementary breathing, so that as you exhale you send your breath into your partner's third eye chakra. Pause as your partner inhales the breath and exhales it back into your third eye, creating another energy circuit. Repeat as many times as you like.

Lips and tongue massage

Otherwise known as kissing! Sadly, often kissing is one of the first pleasures to fall by the wayside in a long-term relationship, yet it is one of the most sensuous pleasures a couple can enjoy. The mouth and lips are among the most sensitive areas of the body. A kiss can spark up hidden erotic desire, or just quickly connect you to an intimate space with your partner. There are many different types of kisses, ranging from tight-lipped to erotic. In India and China the latter type is considered to be the ultimate experience in love-making. It is an amazing exchange of intimacy and trust.

If you're suffering from a lack of libido, therefore, experiment with your lips by licking, sucking, and kissing. Explore every part of your partner's body with your lips and tongue. Eyelids, ears, and neck are especially sensitive. Suck on the fingers and toes. Explore their whole body, leaving the genitals till the very end.

Try experimenting with temperatures—suck on an ice cube before you start kissing—or put a drop of peppermint oil on your tongue before exploring your partner's genitals. They should feel a tingling sensation. There are many different techniques you can learn, but I personally advocate tuning in to your partner and using your intuition. You'll be able to perceive the subtle ways in which they communicate to you what they enjoy and what they don't.

A couple of things to bear in mind when you kiss ...
According to Tantric thought, a women's upper lip is linked to her clitoris by nerves, and the lower lip of a man is linked to his penis. Shiatsu, on the other hand, links the upper lip to the sexual system and holds that pressure on the upper lip stimulates sexual desire.

Pelvic bouncing

This exercise charges your body with sexual energy and is a great way to prepare yourself for Tantric sex. As you become more practiced, try to visualize a constant circuit of silver or gold light moving up the length of your back, over the top of your head, and then down your front to your navel as you bounce. Pelvic bouncing is very powerful. When you first start practicing it, it can trigger a fit of the giggles or sometimes make you cry. This is good, since it provides a release for some of the energy that's stuck in this area. Keep going with it at your own pace. And if you get nothing else out of pelvic bouncing, it will exercise your gluteus maximus …which means it firms up your bottom!

- Lie on your back with your knees bent and feet flat on the floor or bed, a hip width apart.
- Allow your arms to rest by your side, and relax your neck, jaw, and shoulders.
- Lift your pelvis from the floor or bed and bounce it up and down. Choose your own speed, but try to get a rhythm going. It might seem difficult at first, but it becomes easier with practice. Bounce for as long as you like until you feel the energy flowing.

The pc pump

In Tantric teaching the pubococcygeus (PC) muscle helps shoot the energy up the spine. It contracts involuntarily during orgasm, but if you learn to contract the muscle slowly and consciously, you will enjoy stronger orgasms. Experienced tantric practitioners say they can reach orgasm by just contracting the muscle. Once you have mastered the breathing exercise opposite, you can take it a stage further by contracting the PC muscle (as if you're trying to stop yourself peeing), holding your breath for a count of six, and then bearing down when you exhale. It will definitely have an effect on your love life within a few months if you practice it for several minutes a day.

Energetic breathing

You can use this breathing exercise just to play around with energy, and later on you can use it when you are enjoying Tantric sex with your partner. At first you might not feel anything, but don't worry—keep trying, as eventually you will become more in tune with the energy moving around your body. Some people say that this feels like a tingling sensation, others are aware of a warmth, or ripples, or a fluttering feeling like the touch of a butterfly's wings.

- Find somewhere comfortable and quiet. Lie on your back and breathe steadily. As you breathe in, contract your PC muscle (see opposite).
- While breathing in and contracting the muscle, visualize your breath moving up your body to the top of your head.
- Breathe out, release your PC muscle and feel your breath flowing outward.

Fully-clothed orgasm

This is normally known as the "firebreath orgasm" and the technique will enable you to achieve orgasm with your clothes on and just from breathing. No touching! It takes quite a bit of practice, but before too long, you should definitely feel something, albeit just a sensual tingling. Keep at it, however. Most people feel very calm and centered after doing this exercise.

- Lie on your back with your knees bent and feet flat on the floor, a hip width apart.
- Breathe through your mouth and visualize or imagine breathing in energy or gold or silver light from your base chakra (see page 27).
- With each inhalation, tighten your pelvic floor. Keeping it held tight, move up into the sacral chakra and breathe the energy or light into it.
- Repeat the whole process through all the chakras— sacral to solar plexus, solar plexus to heart, heart to throat, throat to third eye, and third eye to crown. (Some people find that they begin to shake or that their back starts to arch. Don't worry—this is just the energy flowing through your body. You will be feeling good by now, so just go with it!)
- When you are ready, bring the energy back to your navel area and relax.

Ring muscles

The ring muscles are the muscles around the mouth, eyes, nostrils, anus, genitals, and perineum. When the ring muscles contract and relax harmoniously, the body is filled with energy. If this is out of rhythm or destabilized by stress, sickness, or tension, the body's energy is depleted. You can contract these muscles to help increase the body's energy and stimulate the internal organs. This, in turn, will increase sexual energy.

• Contract the mouth: suck the cheeks in and relax 40 times.
• Contract the eyes: blink your eyes fast while looking around the room for about a minute. This wakes the body up, especially the nerves, improves eyesight, and opens up the pelvic floor.
• Contract and relax the anus: this energizes the body, strengthens the connection to all the ring muscles of the body, and boosts sexual energy.
• Contract and release the perineum and vagina: this boosts and contains sexual energy, increases the libido, and strengthens the pelvic floor.
• Perform a full body contraction: contract and relax all the ring muscles simultaneously 40 times. This strengthens and energizes the whole body and increases sexual energy.

It takes two

Exploring energy with your partner can be fun as well as sexy. If you take the time to do this exercise, you should begin to see a difference in the quality of your sexual relationship right away.

• Cuddle together like spoons, with one of you hugging the other from behind. You can do this sitting up or lying down. If the man is behind the woman, he should put his hand over hers, or vice versa.
• Breathe in unison. Visualize breathing in and out into each chakra (see page 27), starting at the base, then moving up through to the solar plexus, heart, throat, third eye, and crown chakras.
• Start to become aware of the sensations in your body; you may experience warmth or a tingling sensation. Relax as much as you can, and enjoy the feeling.

After practicing the exercises above, you should feel a little more in tune with your own body as well as your partner's. You should have woken up your sleeping sexual energy and strengthened your sexual partnership. So now try some sexual positions that are known for helping to increase intimacy, strengthening your libido, and healing your body.

sexual energy: a Taoist perspective

It is not just Tantra that utilizes sexual energy. Taoism—along with many other spiritual disciplines—also involves the study and teaching of special secret sexual energy techniques to promote health, longevity, and spiritual fulfilment.

According to Taoist thought, women lose very little energy during sex, while men deplete their energy every time they ejaculate. Taoist practice includes exercises and recommends dietary regimes and herbal remedies to help energize and harmonize the body. Sexual energy is believed to provide nourishment for the mind, body, and soul, and if we want to be healthy, our energy must circulate to all parts of our body. If the energy isn't

flowing properly, it opens the door to sickness, disease and tension—and that includes a low or nonexistent libido. It is important to see a low libido not as an isolated problem but as an indication that there are imbalances in the body as a whole.

So sexual energy, according to Taoism, has an impact on our overall health and aging processes. It does this by affecting the hormonal system. When the sex glands are stimulated, they enhance the hormones secreted by other major endocrine glands. Having a healthy balance of sexual energy helps to repair hormonal disturbances, reduces cholesterol, and lowers blood pressure. Taoists believe that hormones should be stimulated naturally by exercise and massage and not via medication. This is especially important for men. According to Western medicine, men naturally replace their semen soon after an orgasm and therefore have a limitless supply. Taoism does not agree, believing that ejaculation causes energy loss and that semen, along with proper hormone balance, requires a lot of energy to replace. Thus too much sex can leave a man feeling tired, prone to illness, and irritable. Consequently some men might find that their libido improves just by having less sex, so that their body has enough time to regenerate.

Taoists believe that a balanced sexuality can enhance creativity and actually help you to fulfill your dreams. But just as balanced sexual energy is good for emotional well-being, sexual imbalances can cloud the mind with distorted thoughts and unusual desires. They have also developed many techniques to increase sexual energy—sexual reflexology is just one of them. The Taoists refer to sexual intercourse as "healing love," which is why they prescribe certain positions to help heal the body in some way. They believe this works because they regard sex as a form of ecstatic acupressure, since the parts of the body that are most commonly involved in arousal—genitals, hands, mouth, eyes, ears—possess many different meridian points. Sometimes, it is hard to take these exercises seriously, but they are fun to try nontheless and really can help with the libido—however much you're laughing when you do them!

The tao genital massage

The penis and vagina have meridian points, which, if massaged properly, re-energize the glands that help to increase libido. In this exercise, also called the "set of nine exercises," the man penetrates his partner in a series of 90 strokes in order to massage his penis and her vagina evenly. This stimulates the genital reflexology points and hence promotes general well-being as well as a healthy libido. It is also supposed to delay the aging process, as sexual reflexology stimulates the growth hormones that counteract it. So why not try it? If only to look younger!

- The man places the tip of his penis in his partner's vagina and then withdraws nine times. He then thrusts the whole penis into the vagina once.
- He follows this with eight shallow strokes using only the tip and two deep strokes with the entire penis, then seven shallow strokes followed by three deep ones, and so on until he reaches one shallow stroke followed by nine deep ones.

Sexual healing positions

If your priority is to learn about a variety of positions, the *Kama Sutra* offers a wide range of interesting and sometimes acrobatic ones to try; however, the positions described below have been known for many thousands of years to help the sexual healing process. Energy circulates differently around our body, depending on the position we are in. Certain positions increase the energy flow between you and your partner by matching up particular parts of the body, and in this way you create simple energy circuits. Sexual healing positions put pressure on the reflexology points of the penis and vagina, which then stimulates the different organs. For example, the missionary position allows many similar body parts to touch or be close to each other; it enables kissing to continue; and it facilitates eye gazing and chakra alignment, so energy flow in this position is good. Try exploring different positions and feel how the energy flow changes between you.

The positions that I have chosen to include aim to increase the intimacy between a couple or raise sex drive. Some may feel odd at first, but give them time and you *will* notice a difference. If any of them are uncomfortable or painful, simply leave them out.

WOMAN ON TOP

This is one of the easiest positions from a man's point of view if he is trying to control his ejaculations and become multi-orgasmic. This is because he can relax more easily in this position and concentrate on the energy moving up his spine. The great thing for the woman is that she can control how much of the penis enters her vagina, enabling her to guide the penis to her G-spot. The clitoris can also be stimulated easily in this position, allowing the woman to enjoy orgasm during sexual intercourse.

This is a good position for
- a woman in the later stages of pregnancy, as it is comfortable for her;
- an older man, since it requires less exertion than other positions;
- men who are not in the best of health;
- empowering the woman, since they are in the "driving seat";
- increasing intimacy, since a couple can maintain eye contact;
- stimulation of the woman's G-spot.

MAN ON TOP

Otherwise known as the "missionary position," and often thought of as the most traditional of positions, this is the one that will no doubt remind women of the times when they were supposed to lie back and endure sex. This is both unfair and unfortunate, as it is actually very passionate, allowing you to maintain eye contact and also kiss while making love. The woman can stroke her partner's spine, helping to draw his energy upward, and the man is able to control his thrusts to satisfy his partner. Its disadvantage is that it makes stimulating the woman's G-spot difficult, but a pillow under her bottom to raise the pelvis can help.

This is a good position for
• being intimate with your partner and being able to stay connected through eye contact;
• energy circulation, since all the chakras are in alignment with your partner's;
• helping the man to have more powerful all-body orgasmic sensations by moving energy up his spine.

MAN FROM BEHIND

This position is called the "congress of the cow" in the *Kama Sutra*, and can be very arousing for both partners. If the woman is angled downward or lying flat, it is relatively easy for the man to reach her G-spot with his penis and for her to experience multiple orgasms. Also, the vagina is very tight in this position, and can be made even tighter if she squeezes her thighs together to contract her PC muscle (see page 112). This helps the man to control the timing of his ejaculation and for the sensation to be more powerful when he orgasms.

This is a good position for
• the woman, since it is one of the easiest and best positions for G-spot stimulation;
• controlling ejaculation

SITTING OPPOSITE EACH OTHER

This position is called *yab-yom* in India (meaning "mother-father") and is the ultimate Tantric position: the man sits cross-legged with the woman astride him, her legs around his back. The idea is that both of you rock your pelvis or at least exercise your PC muscle together (see page 112). This position is best after maybe an hour of foreplay and penetration, when the chakras are awake and energy is flowing freely up the spine. Try to synchronize your breathing

so that you fall into an almost meditative state. This also circulates the energy between you. Some people report experiencing a full body orgasm in this position, when the energy rushes up the spine with further ripples following close behind.

This is a good position for
- maximum spiritual and emotional connection;
- circulating the energy between you;
- e ncouraging a strong sense of intimacy through eye contact.

Healing positions for men

Although the man receives the healing energy in these positions, the woman also gains, as all are helpful for problems with women's sexual organs by stimulating the production of sex hormones and helping correct menstrual difficulties. In all the positions, the man should try to delay orgasm for as long as possible.

POSITION 1

Good for impotence, premature ejaculation, and difficulty achieving an orgasm. It also boosts the libido.
What do we do? The woman lies on her side with her hips facing upward, so that her torso is twisted. The man is above her.

POSITION 2

Good for energizing both of you
What do we do? The woman lies on her back with a large pillow behind her head and shoulders, and her head bent forward. This allows the vagina to curve slightly, thus massaging the right points on the penis. The man is above her.

POSITION 3

Good for strengthening internal organs, especially the kidneys, spleen and liver, and increasing the libido. (According to Chinese medicine, the liver is responsible for the hormonal system, which plays a big part in raising sex drive.)

What do we do? Lie on your side, facing each other. The woman's upper leg should bend backwards slightly, allowing the man's upper leg to come forwards over her lower leg.

POSITION 4

Good for blood pressure problems and blood deficiencies such as anemia, poor blood quality, and blood clots. It also increases the libido.

What do we do? The man lies on his back and the woman is on top on her knees, facing him, but sitting upright. She doesn't move, but instead he thrusts upward from under her.

POSITION 5

Good for lymphatic and circulatory problems, which affect the libido

What do we do? The man lies on his back and the woman sits above him on her hands and knees. Again, the woman should remain as still as she can as the man thrusts upward from under her.

POSITION 6

Good for the libido and bodily healing in general

What do we do? Not an easy one for women! The woman kneels on the bed and then bends backward with her feet under her until her back and head are on the bed (she can use pillows to support her). The man is on top.

DID YOU KNOW..?

It was traditionally recommended that couples practice these positions several times a day, over a long period of time. This is obviously not possible in modern life, but it doesn't mean they won't work. Simply do what you can.

Healing positions for women

Depth of penetration in these positions is important, since it affects different reflexology zones in the vagina. Once the penis is inserted, the woman should move her pelvis so she can stimulate and massage her vagina. The man should try not to ejaculate.

POSITION 1

Good for the pancreas, liver, and kidneys—therefore helping the libido (since the kidneys help sex drive and the liver is responsible for the hormonal system)

What do we do? The woman lies on her back with her legs around the man's thighs (not back or shoulders). The man is above, on his hands and knees. The woman circulates her hips both clockwise and counter-clockwise, and the man should try not to thrust.

Insertion: Only about 1–2 inches. Like this, the penis touches the lung, heart, and pancreas reflexology zones of the vagina.

POSITION 2

Good for the stomach, spleen, female organs, and digestive system

What do we do? The woman lies on her back with her legs around the man's waist and her arms around his neck or shoulders. She circulates her hips both clockwise and counterclockwise and, as before, the man should try not to move too much.

Insertion: The penis should be inserted about half way.

POSITION 3

Good for the kidneys and, by extension, the libido

What do we do? The man lies on his back, and the woman is on her hands and knees with her back toward him. In this position, and if it helps, the woman can hold the penis in her hand for better control. She circulates her hips both clockwise and counterclockwise.

Insertion: Only about 1–2 inches.

POSITION 4

Good for menstrual problems, headaches, energy blockages, poor circulation, and therefore sex drive

What do we do? The man lies on his back and the woman lies at his side supporting herself on one elbow. Her top leg and hip are over the man's body. Once again, she circulates her hips both clockwise and counterclockwise.

Insertion: The woman can hold the penis throughout intercourse, since it is inserted only halfway, and the position is not easy to maintain.

POSITION 5

Good for the nervous system, hormonal system, liver and eyesight. Since it is good for the hormonal system, it is also good for increasing the libido.

What do we do? The man lies on his back, and the woman is on top, on her knees, facing him, but sitting upright. She rotates her hips in both directions and also moves up and down.

Insertion: This alternates between shallow and deep, as the woman moves up and down.

POSITION 6

Good for anaemia and poor circulation. And since it helps with circulation, it is also good for increasing the libido.

What do we do? The woman lies on her back with her legs in the air and her knees on her chest. The man rests on his knees in front of her with his chest pressed against the soles of her feet. The woman circulates her hips counterclockwise and anticlockwise.

Insertion: Insertion is very deep in this position.

Healing hands

Where you put your hands during sex can focus your partner's attention and energy onto that part of the body. Use the hand positions during rest periods when making love. It is best to lie on your side facing each other when doing this, but go with whatever feels most comfortable.

Sacral pump Strengthens the ovaries and semen.
Position: One hand over the other at the base of your partner's spine.

Kidney energy Strengthens sexual energy, life force, and bone marrow.
Position: One hand on each kidney.

Adrenal glands Strengthens the internal organs and increases sex appeal and drive.
Position: One hand to either side of spine at waist level.

Liver and spleen Helps balance the hormones and helps with libido.
Position One hand on top of the other halfway down the back.

Heart and lungs Strengthens blood circulation, erection, vaginal lubrication, and libido.
Position One hand on each lung.

Sacral and C7 Increases sexual energy and libido.
Position One hand on the base of the spine and the other at the base of the neck (C7).

Sacral and crown Improves erection, vaginal lubrication, and women's orgasm.
Position One hand on the base of the spine and the other at the top of the head.

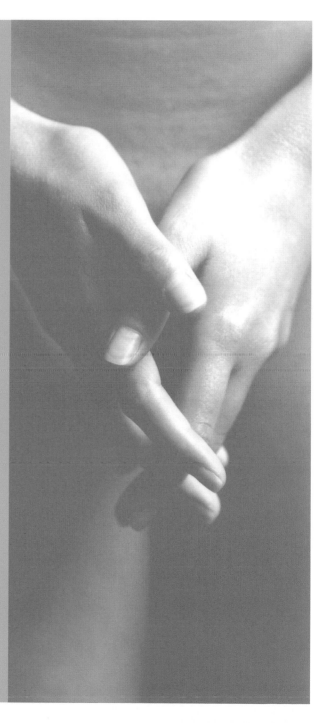

CHAPTER SIX

keeping your sex life alive

long-term love

In a long-term relationship, with all its stresses and strains, from marriage to careers to babies to the menopause, it is perfectly normal to experience problems in the bedroom department at one time or another. If you don't, you're either very lucky or not being entirely honest with yourself.

It is inevitable that the longer you're with someone, the more familiar you become with their body, their ways, and their likes and dislikes. So how do you stop sex from growing less exciting over time? With a little effort and imagination, that's how. If there is love, trust, and respect in your relationship, there is no reason why your sex life can't get better and better the older you get. Read on for some great ideas on how to spice things up.

Erogenous zones

Rediscovering erogenous zones is particularly important for people in long-term relationships who have got stuck in the rut of habitual or speedy sex, which is focused mainly on the genitals rather than

Feng shui for lovers

Create a sacred space where you and your partner can really enjoy sex. Go to town with colors and sumptuous fabrics that conjure up for you the idea of a sacred sex palace or boudoir. Experiment with soft cushions, candles, incense, oil burners, bowls of rose petals, fresh flowers, plates of fruit, feathers—whatever works for you. Some people like to make a circle around the bed with candles, pebbles, crystals, bowls of water or petals, casting a circle and creating a sacred enclosure that protects and embraces your relationship with each other. You can even make an altar in the bedroom as a symbol of the sanctity of your relationship. You can do this by covering a low table, box, or shelf with beautiful fabric, on which you can arrange objects that are sacred to you or to your relationship: flowers, crystals and pictures of you together.

Clear your room of clutter and regularly check that everything you have in there you actually want to keep. If not, get rid of it. Clutter signifies stuck energy, and by clearing the space, you are allowing fresh new energy to circulate. It would be good to have nothing in your room except your bed and the things that make you feel sensual, intimate, and sexual with your partner. Few of us can afford the luxury of having our clothes, books, and other possessions somewhere else entirely, but you can find clever ways to store such items so that they are not obvious. Your room should look as you would have wanted it to look the first

other equally sensitive body bits. Think about how it felt when you first met and every part of you would react to the slightest touch. Finding new zones (that you never knew you had!) can in itself be great fun as well as sexually stimulating. Play around and explore your partner's body until you find the spots that make them tingle. If you're feeling uninspired, here are some ideas:

- the breasts/nipples (for both men and women)
- the mouth, which is one of the most sensitive parts of the body
- the neck and nape of the neck
- the face and ears
- the back and small of the back
- the fingers and palms
- the buttocks
- the perineum
- the inside of the thighs
- the backs of the knees
- the soles of the feet

Magic salt bath ritual

You will need: water, candles, salt, damiana extract, essential oils of ylang-ylang, vanilla, and lavender, almond massage oil and optional soft red lightbulbs or red glass candle holders (for the sacral (sexual) chakra—not to make the bathroom look like a brothel!).

- Add 5 drops of each essential oil and a tablespoon of almond oil to the bath.
- Prepare a salt scrub in a bowl by putting in 1 cup of salt, 30 drops of damiana extract, and a few tablespoons of water. (This is supposed to be rainwater that you collected earlier, but tap water works just as well.)
- Stand in the running bath and take it in turns to rub the salt scrub on each other. This stimulates the circulation and exfoliates the skin, while the damiana increases sexual desire. Take care to avoid the eyes and genitals.
- Slip into the warm water together and give each other a sensual massage.

night you brought your lover home. I know this is easier said than done, but at least keeping it as an aim will help you move farther toward achieving a sacred space where you both can connect spiritually, and where your energy and sexuality are allowed to flow.

Of course, your sacred sexual space does not have to be your bedroom; but wherever it is, keep the energy cleansed by burning sage, sprinkling water scented with your favorite essential oil, or using a space-clearing spray filled with flower essences. This will keep it free from negative energy while preserving the energy you have tried to create. Aim to cleanse your sacred space every time you intend to use it, recharging it each time with erotic union and connection. Treat this space as if it were your temple. Open the windows to air the room, and burn incense every day. Try to work something into your daily routine that will help you to do this, so that it becomes a habit and is not hard to keep up.

When you have a baby...

Sex drive can be affected greatly during pregnancy. Some women say it increases, while others feel no desire at all to have sex. It seems that every pregnancy is different. Those who do enjoy a higher sex drive, however, notice that orgasms are easier to achieve and more intense, possibly as a result of increased lubrication and blood supply to the genitals. Low sex drive can be linked to many things during pregnancy and in early motherhood, including exhaustion; lack of self-confidence; stitches or pain; fearing that your vagina has stretched; feeling out of sorts with your body; fear of waking the baby; fear of getting pregnant again; confusion caused by your new role as a mother; postnatal depression; and sore or leaking breasts. With a list so long, it's not surprising that men

get confused by their partner's physical and emotional fluctuations, including hidden chemical changes her pheromones.

Most people think their sex drive will return to normal straight after having a baby, but this is often not the case. Once the baby is born, women who breast-feed produce the hormone prolactin, which reduces the sex drive. It's possibly nature's way of helping to prevent another pregnancy so soon after the previous one. After the initial three months of breast-feeding, prolactin levels slowly start to return to normal. Women who bottle-feed their babies stop secreting prolactin within eight days of giving birth, but that does not mean they should expect their libido to return to normal this quickly!

HOW CAN YOU HELP YOURSELF?

Many women allow themselves to eat whatever they like while they are pregnant, promising themselves they'll get back into shape after the birth. This is easier said than done, and it takes hard work and determination. You can become so tired from caring for a new baby, and so fed up with how you look and feel, that you fall into the trap of comfort-eating. Body image can be a real problem for new mothers, and it is therefore vital to take care of your diet and try to fit exercise into your weekly routine, even if it is just going for long brisk walks pushing the buggy every day. Try to incorporate some hills into the walks, too, as this will improve your muscle tone.

Make an effort with your appearance, both for

As you get older...

From the way in which it is portrayed in the media, one could be forgiven for thinking that sex is the province of the young. This is not true. There are more people of retirement age living full, healthy, active lives than ever before. Sexually, however, there are many hormonal changes that may affect the libido and lead to problems in a relationship.

yourself and for your partner, and if your body image is one of the things that are preventing you from enjoying your sex life again, talk it through. Try to work out a goal, and get him involved, so that he can help you achieve it, even if it is just looking after the baby while you exercise. Take it one step at a time, and try out some of the tips on page 138. Things will slowly return to normal.

One of the biggest passion killers when you have children is tiredness due to broken nights and lack of sleep. If you have small children, try power-napping when they have their nap—15 minutes' snoozing is an instant recharge.

THE MENOPAUSE

The female menopause, which usually occurs when a woman is between 45 and 55 years old, is caused by the gradual loss of estrogen. It is the lowered estrogen levels and the ovaries' slow loss of egg follicles that can weaken sex drive, especially if the woman is also feeling stressed. Some women report that sex is not so pleasurable after the menopause because of vaginal dryness making intercourse painful, or difficulty in reaching an orgasm.

If you are experiencing vaginal dryness, a water-based lubricant or pessaries will alleviate this and help put zest back into your sex life. Dietary changes (see page 46) can also raise estrogen levels. Soy, for example, not only will stimulate your libido but will help with symptoms of the menopause too. Many women also find acupuncture (see page 54) and homeopathy (see page 58) very effective at this time. Healthy living—plenty of exercise, a good diet and not too much alcohol or caffeine—will certainly help alleviate the symtoms.

However, the menopause doesn't affect all women this way. Some report an increase in libido after the menopause, and others find it liberating, because for the first time in their life there is no need to worry about contraception or unwanted pregnancy.

THE ANDROPAUSE

The andropause ("male menopause") occurs between the ages of 40 and 55. It is probably best known as the "midlife crisis." Although many medical experts deny its existence, there are physical symptoms, which include bodily changes, tiredness, a change in attitude or mood (usually increasing irritability), excessive sweating, hot flashes—and often an overwhelming desire to buy a little red sports car!

At this time men often question their direction in life, their values, and their accomplishments. They can also experience reduced sexual desire and potency, difficulties with erections and ejaculation, reduced fertility, various urinary problems, and prostate

Does size matter?

Many men are obsessed with the size of their penis, believing that if only it were larger, sex would be better—hence the popularity of surgical enlargements. According to many Eastern teachings, however, it is not the length but the strength of the penis that is important. In terms of libido, lack of self-confidence is a killer—it cannot be stressed too often that the most important thing is not size or shape, but to know that your partner loves you for who you are. Sexual confidence is strongest where there is love and mutual respect in the relationship.

problems, which can weaken the libido. Often the physical difficulties that older men experience with erections can be attributed to a slowing-down of testosterone production (see page 25). This can be exacerbated by stress, obesity, smoking, depression, diet, drugs, alcohol, and heredity, and often adjustments in diet and lifestyle can make a world of difference.

It is possible for men to have a good sex drive even when they are in their 80s, but they must exercise their PC muscle (see page 112)—otherwise it becomes weak and wasted like any other muscle. The penis can actually withdraw if it is not used regularly and older men who are less sexually active can experience this. Exercising your PC muscle strengthens the erection as well as allowing stronger orgasms. It is also very important for the health of the prostate, as the contractions stimulate and massage the prostate gland.

Viagra: the myth

Countless couples experiencing difficulty have opted for the drug Viagra, but there are serious downsides to this approach. Let's just take a look at how it works and why it's better for couples to seek healthier alternatives.

In 1998 Viagra was launched as a treatment for male impotence. Many normally functioning men thought, and still think, that Viagra would help them achieve stronger erections than they already had, or would rid them of inhibitions. This is not the case. It helps men to have erections, but does not increase their libido, or desire.

When a man receives sexual stimulation, nitric oxide is released locally in the penis. Viagra enhances the smooth muscle relaxant effects of nitric oxide and blocks enzymes that normally stop chemicals from initiating erections. Blood then flows into the penis, causing an erection. However, there are now concerns that it has serious side effects, such as headaches; dizziness; flushing; upset stomach; urinary tract infections; visual changes, including increased sensitivity to light; and low blood pressure or strokes in high-risk people when used with nitrates and other heart medication.

Exercises for a stronger erection

This Taoist exercise strengthens and improves muscle control and will work wonders for your confidence as it begins to have the desired affect. Of course, you don't have to do this in front of your partner, but it does give you both a good laugh!

- Hang a flannel or small cloth over your erect penis.
- Contract your genital muscles and see how far you can raise it. Release and repeat a few more times.
- As you improve, move on to a heavier cloth or small towel.
- You can also try gently squeezing the base of your penis repeatedly until it is very hard, to increase the blood flow to its tissues. Practise this for a few minutes every day.

'My concern about Viagra is that it technologizes sex and leaves people with the impression that it is just about a firm erection... Yes, Viagra is going to speak to getting more blood into the penis but it will not speak to getting passion and compassion into the heart.'
Dr Jerald Bain, Mount Sinai Hospital.

Hormone replacement therapy

HRT, as it is better known, is an orthodox treatment for the symptoms of the menopause, including vaginal dryness and loss of libido. It introduces synthetic hormones into the bloodstream to counteract estrogen depletion, a symptom of the menopause. It comes in the form of implants, tablets, and creams. However, HRT remains controversial, as there can be serious side effects. It has been linked to an increased risk of cancer, especially breast cancer, and there is evidence to suggest that it also contributes to the risk of cardiovascular disease

HORMONE LIBIDO ENHANCERS

Hormone supplements can be taken to boost sex drive, but hormones need to be treated with respect and caution and can be dangerous if used wrongly. Tiny amounts can cause big reactions, both good and bad, and some scientists believe that hormone supplementation can cause some kinds of cancers. There may be instances when taking a hormone supplements is medically advisable, but not unless you are deficient in that hormone. Always seek medical advice first.

PHEROMONES

Chemical copies of human pheromones can now be obtained via mail order, and these are generally safe to use. You can add them to your own favorite unatomized perfume or aftershave (they will not affect its smell) or put them into a candle. Women with a low sex drive can dab a male pheromone extract under their nose or put it in their partner's aftershave. Likewise, men can add a female sex pheromone to their partner's perfume. However, be warned that these pheromones might attract other people, not just your partner!

Female pheromones can be smelled over a distance, such as across a large room, but a woman needs to be within close proximity to a male pheromone to pick up the scent. Use the pheromone scent at least every other day and wear it for at least six hours before washing it off. Some people notice results within days, but for others it takes about six weeks.

Age is only a number

The hormonal changes that occur as people age are not the only thing they have to contend with. The other big problem is sexual confidence. In Western society we are led to believe that youth and beauty are synonymous and to age is to lose your attractiveness.

Women are now spending more on plastic surgery, facial treatments, anti-wrinkle creams, and hair dyes than ever before. But how much of this is culturally imposed? In traditional Aboriginal cultures, older women are seen as very sexually attractive and will often have partners who are much younger than they. Western women need to rediscover the fact that they are still potent sexual beings, no matter how their bodies are changing.

Ovarian breathing

According to Taoist thought, the ovaries are a powerful source of energy. If you can tap into this, it can revitalize the nervous system and keep you looking and feeling young and healthy. Try the following exercise.

• Visualize energy coming up your spine. If it helps, imagine the energy as a gold light.
• Bring the energy up to your head.
• Then bring the energy down through the tongue, heart and solar plexus, and finally store it in the navel.

DID YOU KNOW...

The number of times a couple has sex halves after they have been together more than a year.

Top tips for keeping your sex life alive...

Being sexy is a state of mind, so visualize yourself sexy. Keep fit, so you can feel good about your body and so that you can be flexible for sex!

Dress sexily for each other. Even after years of marriage, it is important still to care about your appearance and make an effort for your partner. After all, if you don't, why should they?

Try out new things together, such as Tantric sex, massage, and aphrodisiac foods—besides helping to increase your libido, they will give you a shared experience.

Vary where and when you have sex. Don't keep it just in the bedroom. Initiate sex when your partner least expects it, and be a little spontaneous.

Go on "dates" and trips away. This not only will help you relax—often the key to good sex—but will offer a welcome change of scenery and a chance to get away from it all, even if just for a night.

Have fun. Flirting with each other will take you back to when you first met and fell in love. It will help to keep the sexual energy alive even after years of marriage.

And finally...
a word on kissing

"The kiss is the gateway to bliss and amorous experience. The kiss provokes erotic ardor, agitates the heart, and is an incitation to the natural gift of self." *Kama Sutra*

Kissing creates a powerful energy, and it is strange that something so erotic, sensual, and romantic often becomes the first casualty in a long-term relationship. It is often a sign that intimacy has been lost, and it is very important that you work at re-introducing it. So next time you go to peck your partner hello, give them a long sexy kiss instead.

resources

resources

USA
The National Association for Holistic Aromatherapy
4509 Interlake Ave N.# 233
Seattle
WA 98103-6773
206 547 2164
www.naha.org/
For information and advice.

Healing Tao and USA
PO Box 24
Lodi, NJ 07644 0024
973 777 4442
www.healingtaousa.com
For Taoist healing, teaching and products.

Homeopathic American Association of Sex Educators, Counselors and Therapists (AASECT)
PO Box 5488
Richmond
VA 23220 0488
804 644 3288
www.aasect.org/
For counseling and advice.

Athena Institute for Women's Wellness
1211 Braefield Road
Chester Springs, PA 19425
(+1) 610 827 2200
www.athenainstitute.com
For synthetic copies of male and female pheromones.

Educational Service
2124B Kittredge Street
Berkeley, CA 94704
510 649 0294
www.homeopathic.com
For advice and products.

Humanetics Corporation
12200 Middleset Road, Suite 500,
Eden Prairie, MN 55344
(+1) 952 937 7660
www.humaneticscorp.com
For pheromones and DHEA hormone creams.

Bioforce USA
437 Route 295
Chatham, NY 12037
518 392 8737
www.bioforceusa.com
For herbs, vitamins, flower essences and books.

Nelson Bach USA
Wilmington Technology Park
100 Research Drive
Wilmington
MA 01887 4406
1 800 319 9151
www.bachessences.com
For Flower Remedies.

Pacific Sensuals
14145 Beverly Glen Boulevard
Los Angeles, CA 90024
(+1) 310 286 1183
For pheromone candles, massage oils, and other sensual products.

Solgar Vitamins
500 Willow Tree Road
Leonia, New Jersey 07605
1 877 SOLGAR 4
www.solgar.com
For vitamins and herbs.

Whole Spectrum
6710 Benjamin Road Suite 700
Tampa
FL 33634
813 886 9698
www.aromatherapyproducts.info/
For aromatherapy products.

AUSTRALIA & NZ
Australian Acupuncture Association
P.O. Box 5142
West End
Brisbane 4101
(+61) 07 3846 5866
For information and therapists.

Australian Naturopathic Practitioners
1st Floor, 609 Camberwell Road,
Camberwell
VIC 3124
(+61) 03 9889 0488
For information and therapists.

Association of Massage Therapists
18A Spit Road
Mosman
NSW 1088
Australia

New Zealand Homeopathic Association
P.O. Box 2929, Auckland
(+64) 09 303 3124
For information and products.

CANADA
Chinese Medicine and Acupunture Association
154 Wellington Street, London
Ontario N6B 2K8
(+1) 519 642 1970
For advice and therapists.

Canadian Natural Health Product Association
550 Alden Road, Suite 505,
Markham, Ontario L3R 6AB
(+1) 905 479 6939
For information.

Shiatsu School of Canada Inc.
547 College Street, Toronto
Ontario M6G 1A9
(+1) 416 323 1818
For information on treatments and practitioners.

Canadian Center for Stress and Wellbeing
141 Adelaide Street West, Suite
1506, Toronto, Ontario M5H 3L5
(+1) 416 363 6204
For information and advice on therapies and treatments.

UNITED KINGDOM
Diamond Light Tantra
P.O. Box 38204
London NW3 6Y2
www.diamondlighttantra.com
For Tantra workshops.

The General Council of Consultant Herbalists
31 King Edwards Road
Swansea SA1 4LL
00 44 (0)1792 655 886
For information and advice.

International Flower Essence Repertoire
Achamore House, Isle of Gigha,
Argyll, Scotland PA41 7AD
00 44 (0)1583 505 835
www.healingflowers.com
For bottled flower essences from around the world.

further reading

Boosting the Male Libido Zoltan Rona **The Ancient Wisdom of Chinese Tonic Herbs** Ron Teeguarden **Cooking for Healthy Healing** Linda Page **Elixirs, Tonics, and Teas** Jeff Stein and Edgar Veytia **Erotic Massage** Kenneth Ray Stubbs **How Big is Big?** Anne Hooper and Jeremy Holford **Increase Your Sex Drive** Dr Sarah Brewer **Natural Aphrodisiacs** Fiona Marshall **Sensual Aromatherapy** Nitya Lacroix **Sexopedia** Anne Hooper **Sextasy** Caroline Aldred **Sex with Spirit** Michelle Pauli **Sexual Reflexology** Mantak Chia and William Wei **Shiatsu for Lovers** Nathan Strauss **Tantra Between the Sheets** Val Sampson **Tantric Sexuality** Richard Craze **The Kama Sutra: The Essence of India** Bret Norton **The Magical and Ritual Use of Aphrodisiacs** Richard Alan Miller

picture acknowledgements

Key: ABPL = Anthony Blake Photo Library; BAL = Bridgeman Art Library
page: 9 Alinari / BAL; 11 Archives Charmet / BAL; 12 Steve McCurry / Magnum Photos; 18 Gueorgui Pinkhassov / Magnum Photos; 31 Science and Society Picture Library; 50(l) Rex Butcher / The Garden Picture Library; 50 (r) Steven Morris / ABPL; 51 Tim Imrie / ABPL; 53 The Garden Picture Library / IPS; 56 Archives Charmet / BAL; 61 Clive Nichols; 63 Clive Nichols; 66 Clive Nichols; 78 Free Library, Philadelphia / BAL; 79 The Stapleton Collection / BAL; 85 Anthony Blake / ABPL; 87 Sian Irvine / ABPL; 92 Joff Lee / ABPL; 97 Joff Lee / ABPL; 98 Martin Brigdale / ABPL; 99 Georgia Glynn Smith / ABPL; 107 Brooklyn Museum of Art / BAL; 108 Dinodia Picture Agency, Bombay / BAL; 128 Nat Herz / BAL; 132 ER Productions / Corbis; 134 Science and Society Picture Library; 135 Royalty Free / Corbis; 136 Nikos Economopoulos / Magnum Photos.

index

one last thought...

Passionate, energetic sex can burn up to 500 calories per hour – the same as a gentle jog or cycle. Now if that's not enough to tempt you into bed, nothing is!

Oriah Mountain Dreamer